A TASTE OF
WASHINGTON

Favorite Recipes from the Evergreen State

by Michele Morris

foreword by Andy Perdue

FARCOUNTRY
PRESS

✃ For Jenny ✃

ISBN 10: 1-56037-602-3
ISBN 13: 978-1-56037-602-6

© 2014 by Farcountry Press
Food photography and text © 2014 by Michele Morris

Back cover photo © 2014 Charles Gurche
Pages ii-iii photo © 2014 Stemilt Growers LLC, www.stemilt.com

For more information about our books, write Farcountry Press,
P.O. Box 5630, Helena, MT 59604; call (800) 821-3874; or visit
www.farcountrypress.com.

Library of Congress Cataloging-in-Publication Data on file.

Created, produced, and designed in the United States.
Printed in China.

18 17 16 15 14   1 2 3 4 5

contents

chapter 1: Breakfast & Brunch

chapter 2: Appetizers & Snacks

chapter 3: Salads & Sides

chapter 4: Soups & Stews

chapter 5: Main Courses

chapter 6: Desserts & Sweet Treats

acknowledgments

Thank you to the chefs, restaurateurs, innkeepers, farmers, ranchers, fishermen, winemakers, and all of the other fine food producers across the state of Washington who made this book possible. Their passion about their food and their creativity in the kitchen were inspiring, and without their willingness to share, this cookbook would not have been possible. The incredible recipes from these venues, featuring the very best of what the state has to offer, are what make a cookbook like this so exciting to work on.

Creating a cookbook can be solitary, and the sheer amount of food can overwhelm even those with the heartiest appetites. Fortunately, I have many friends who are talented home cooks who were willing to help on this project, and I thank all of them for their support. Karen Adkins, Sharon Bayliss, Susan Bechler, Melanie Buscher, Kirsten Hall, Tai Hernandez, Sarah Hubregsen, Laura James, Teresa Leede, Lisa Maney, Sharon Mehrtens, Susie Moss and her son Steven Moss, Wendy Peterson, Christy Porter and her son Reed Porter, Lori Reed, Florine Richardson, Kasey Rudolph, Ian Shaw, Ruth Stemler, and Julie Wunderlich all spent hours in the kitchen with me helping during recipe testing, assisting in photo shoots, cleaning an enormous amount of dishes, and in general, making my job as a cookbook author a lot more fun. I sent them home with the cooked dishes as "payment" for their time and efforts, so I never had to worry about food going to waste, something that's very important to me.

Thank you to Whole Foods, Seattle Fish Company, and Taylor Shellfish, all of whom were a tremendous help in acquiring the freshest seafood, including a live geoduck and a gorgeous octopus, for testing the recipes in the cookbook. Thanks to Pike Place Market—after one visit to that iconic

place, I had more ideas and inspiration for the book than any author could ask for. I owe Dick Kirkpatrick special thanks for sharing elk with me from his annual hunting trip.

I want to thank the staff at Farcountry Press. My editor, Will Harmon, was always there when I needed a question answered and he provided valuable input for this book, as did publisher Linda Netschert. Shirley Machonis is a gifted designer and worked with me to ensure that the best of my photos made it into the final book. Thanks in advance to the marketing staff, who I know from previous experience will be invaluable in marketing the cookbook after its release.

Finally, I owe a very special thank you to my husband and biggest cheerleader, Greg. His support allows me to pursue my passion of a career in food and wine, and for that I am eternally grateful.

foreword

by Andy Perdue

Washington is a state of incredible beauty, diversity, and bounty.

In just a few hours, you can drive from wheat land to shrub-steppe to sky-piercing mountains to a water-surrounded metropolis to fjords and to rain forests before arriving at the world's longest beach. And those are just the highlights.

Washington is a breadbasket for chefs seeking fresh local ingredients. Consider this: Washington state is first in the nation in producing apples, blueberries, red raspberries, processed carrots, chickpeas, juice grapes, hops, pears, mint oil, sweet cherries, fresh peas, and processed sweet corn. Additionally, the state is in the top ten in the country in crops such as asparagus, apricots, wine grapes, nectarines, onions, potatoes, dried peas, lentils, tart cherries, plums, wheat, barley, cranberries, strawberries, fresh sweet corn, and peaches.

These are just the big crops. One small farm in the Columbia Basin town of Eltopia actually grows more than 300 different crops, including more than thirty varieties of eggplants.

While impressive, this expansive view of farming across the state doesn't even include the amazing riches we receive from the sea. Our oysters are famous throughout the world, as are our Dungeness crab, our salmon, and our clams (including the famed geoduck, one of the world's largest clams, for which you'll find a recipe herein).

In addition, dairies provide milk for drinking and cheese production, and ranchers in central and eastern Washington raise cattle and sheep for meat.

Washington's wine industry is firmly No. 2 in the country. Though far behind California in total production, Washington's 50,000 acres of vineyards and more than 800 wineries compete on a quality level with the best of Napa Valley and Sonoma County. From Riesling to Cabernet Sauvignon, Washington has proven its worth in the world of wine.

For brewers, Washington provides all the key ingredients, and the inspiration for the modern craft brewing movement can be traced to the eastern Washington city of Yakima, where Grant's Brewery opened in 1982—the nation's first brewpub since Prohibition. In short, Washington provides an amazing level of abundance by any measure.

The key to Washington's diversity is the rugged Cascade Mountains, which bisect the state east from west. Mount Rainier, Mount Adams, Mount Baker, and Mount St. Helens—which famously blew its top in 1980 and continues to cause occasional volcanic excitement—highlight the range, which keeps most of the moisture in the western part of the state.

Seattle's notorious rain (which is only half of what Miami gets, by the way) is caused primarily because the clouds arriving from the Pacific Ocean are stopped by the Cascades. While this provides ample precipitation for farming around Puget Sound, it also keeps the east side of the state perpetually arid. The heart of Washington wine country—a three-hour drive east of Seattle—receives only six to eight inches of rain per year.

And this is where the Cascades provide a vital service. The snow that falls in the mountains acts as a reservoir that feeds such rivers as the Yakima and Columbia. These rivers are the lifeblood of Washington agriculture. Without them, little could grow, but with them, hundreds of thousands of acres of land are used to grow nearly every crop we could possibly consider.

The result of this remarkable climate? The stunning quality and quantity of fresh ingredients available here combined with the exciting, diverse, and laid-back attitude of the Pacific Northwest work together to attract many of the world's top chefs, putting the food scene here in the major leagues right along with Vancouver, Portland, and San Francisco. For the lucky diners, the result is a never-ending opportunity to savor the bounty of the region as served up by the creative chefs who live and work here.

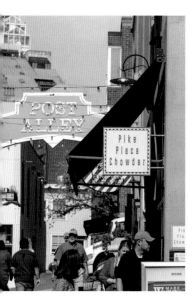

Here in your hands, Michele Morris' cookbook does a beautiful job of capturing the amazing breadth and depth of Washington's agricultural bounty from a culinary point of view. While many cookbook authors tend to focus on the greater Seattle area (because that is where the majority of the population lives and, thus, where the chefs are), Michele has traveled a winding trail that will transport you to the best food in every corner of the Evergreen State.

Washington is a treasure trove of succulent and savory wonder; let Michele be your guide.

Andy Perdue is the wine columnist for the Seattle Times *and editor and publisher of* Great Northwest Wine, *a news and information company (greatnorthwestwine.com).*

introduction

For as long as I can remember, back to my very early years, I have loved to cook. I learned to cook the basics at my mom's side as a young child. By the time I was fourteen, I shooed her out of the house for the day and made her an entire Chinese dinner, complete with homemade wonton soup, from scratch, for her birthday. When I was in college, my room-mates and I would create special meals for our friends, despite our frugal college budgets. And as a young adult I learned how to throw just about every kind of dinner party imaginable, from simple to spectacular. What enabled me to cook so well, even at a young age, without any formal training? In a word: cookbooks. I began collecting cookbooks as a kid, and by the time I was in my thirties, had amassed a collection of about 400. Today, although I cook largely my own creations from scratch, I still can't resist a brilliant cookbook—one with tested and reliable recipes, gorgeous food photos, a bit of a story to tell, and something new to taste.

Certainly a broad collection of creative recipes using the very best ingredients is of utmost importance in a cookbook. As I began research-ing which Washington chefs and venues I wanted to include in this book, I met chefs with an astounding gift for creativity, along with some fierce commitments: to the quality of food they serve at their restaurants or inns, to their insistence on using fresh and seasonal ingredients, and to their passionate support of the local farmers, ranchers, fishermen (and fisherwomen), orchardists, vintners, gardeners, and producers who supply them.

People tell me all the time how important it is to have pictures of the finished dishes in a cookbook, and so I've worked hard to capture each and every one for you in this collection. My food styling and food photography skills are largely self-taught, yet very important to me. I took great pride in putting these images together, and I hope they whet your appetite and lure you into the kitchen as you peruse the pages of this book.

The food scene in Washington is widely regarded as one of the most exciting in our country. Farmers grow everything from apples—

60 percent of the nation's production—to grapes and mushrooms and lentils. Ranchers turn out some of the best pork, lamb, and beef. There is ample opportunity for hunting wild game such as elk and venison. Washington's wine country, established just after the repeal of Prohibition, is booming. And with a seemingly endless availability of some of the best seafood in the world, it's no wonder chefs here are inspired.

In this collection of recipes from the finest chefs at some of the best venues across the state, you'll find everything from a simple salad made with local arugula to a decadent cake made with chocolate from Seattle chocolatier Theo. I've included recipes from some of the most well-known James Beard award–winning chefs, as well as from some of the best home cooks turned innkeepers. I've also tested all the recipes to ensure the portions and instructions work for a home cook, and where needed, steps were simplified. Rest assured, however, that throughout the book, the chefs' visions and recipes remain intact.

Those recipes include intriguing dishes like sautéed geoduck or a sherbet made from pine needles (one of my favorite recipes in the book), but also classic fare such as pancakes, fried Walla Walla onions (irresist-ible), roasted halibut, short ribs, and crème brûlée. No matter what the recipe, I know you'll be impressed with the incredible combination of flavors brought together into a single bite. Enjoy this taste of Washington!

guidelines for recipes

- ❧ All temperatures are listed in degrees Fahrenheit.

- ❧ When a recipe calls for something to be pureed, you may use either an immersion stick blender or a traditional blender. While stick blenders are easier when dealing with hot liquids, keep in mind that they generally don't produce a puree that is as smooth as a traditional blender.

- ❧ When portioning batter for baked goods, an ice cream scoop with a spring release works well to ensure even portions and to easily transfer the batter to muffin tins or molds.

- ❧ Recipes calling for a baking dish were tested using glass baking dishes. Note that substituting a metal baking pan will affect baking time, so check the dish frequently.

- ❧ While not stated explicitly in the instructions, all produce should be thoroughly washed before using it, and onions and garlic should be peeled of their outer papery skin. Look to the instructions or ingredients list to see if other ingredients should be peeled first.

- ❧ Fresh herbs enhance both the taste and the presentation of food and are called for in many of the recipes. Fresh herbs from the garden are cheap and convenient, and most grocery stores sell packaged fresh herbs year-round.

- ❧ Unless otherwise stated, all-purpose flour should be used in any recipes calling for flour. If a recipe calls for cake flour, you may substitute 1 cup of all-purpose flour, less 2 tablespoons, mixed with 2 tablespoons of cornstarch. Pastry flour produces a more tender result, but may be replaced by all-purpose flour.

- ❧ Oats refers to whole rolled oats, not quick cooking oats.

- ❧ Sugar refers to granulated white sugar unless otherwise noted.

❧ You'll find many recipes use heavy cream in the restaurant version of the recipe. For most soups and side dishes, you can substitute half-and-half or milk to reduce calories and fat, although the finished dish will not have the same rich flavor and may not be as thick. In sauces, where the cream is generally used to thicken the sauce, or in baked goods, substitution is not recommended.

❧ Unless otherwise noted, pepper refers to freshly ground black pepper. When a recipe calls for salt, use either kosher salt or sea salt.

❧ Chile peppers lend themselves to a plethora of dishes and almost as many spellings. In this book, *chile* refers to a chile pepper itself or a sauce or oil made from chiles. Spelled as *chili*, it refers to the finished stew or to the spice mixture, chili powder, used in making the stew. The spelling on product labels at your grocer may vary.

❧ Recipes were tested using large eggs.

❧ Fresh eggs are harder to peel when hard cooked, so choose slightly older eggs for any recipes calling for hard cooked eggs.

❧ Breadcrumbs refer to finely ground, dry, unseasoned breadcrumbs unless stated otherwise.

❧ When a recipe calls for stock (chicken, beef, or veal), you may substitute broth.

❧ Nuts may be toasted either in the oven or on the stove. In the oven, spread nuts in a single layer on a baking sheet and bake at 350 degrees until lightly browned and aromatic. On the stove, spread nuts in a single layer in a skillet and cook over medium heat, stirring frequently, until nuts begin to brown and become aromatic. Nuts can burn very quickly once they start browning, so watch closely and do not overcook.

❧ Unless a recipe specifically calls for a certain type of apple, you may use any crisp apple for most recipes.

❧ If serving oysters raw, always shuck fresh oysters just before serving. Pre-shucked oysters may be used in recipes where the oysters will be cooked. When shucking oysters, be sure to use the dull knife-like tool specifically designed for this purpose as using a sharp knife can be dangerous.

❧ To clean mussels, first wash the mussels to remove any outer sand or debris. Next, carefully remove any traces of the beard (the fibrous matter sometimes found sticking out from mussels) by holding the mussel in one hand, grasping the beard, and pulling it towards the hinge end of the mussel to remove it. Discard the beard fibers.

❧ You'll enjoy the best flavor if you use only high-quality, true maple syrup in the recipes calling for it.

Breakfast & Brunch

4 large eggs

1 cup milk

3 tablespoons sugar

1 teaspoon vanilla extract

½ teaspoon salt

1 teaspoon cinnamon

¾ cup flour

6 tablespoons butter

2 tart apples, peeled, cored,
    and sliced

½ cup brown sugar

Serves 6 to 8

Apple Baked Puff Pancake

A HARBOR VIEW INN, ABERDEEN   ❧   INNKEEPER CINDY LONN

The thirty-room estate dating back to 1905 that is now home to A Harbor View Inn boasts water views from every room. This recipe, a favorite of the innkeeper's grandmother, showcases Washington apples and is a guest favorite at the inn. Despite its impressive presentation, it's actually quite easy to make.

Preheat the oven to 425 degrees.

Whisk the eggs, milk, sugar, vanilla, salt, and cinnamon together in a large bowl until well blended. Add the flour and whisk until the batter is smooth.

Place the butter in a 1½- to 2-quart shallow baking dish and place the dish in the oven until the butter is melted, about 5 minutes. Remove the dish from the oven and layer the apple slices in overlapping rows on top of the butter. Return the baking dish to the oven and bake until the apples begin to soften slightly and the butter is bubbling, about 5 minutes.

Remove from the oven and pour the batter over the apples, and then sprinkle with the brown sugar. Bake until puffed and brown, about 20 to 30 minutes. Serve immediately for best flavor and presentation.

¼ cup uncooked quinoa,
  rinsed several times

½ cup water

2 cups oats, divided

1 cup whole wheat flour

1 teaspoon baking soda

1 teaspoon baking powder

2 teaspoons cinnamon

¼ teaspoon salt

¾ cup sugar

¼ cup canola oil

2 eggs

½ cup plain nonfat Greek yogurt

2 cups diced apples
  (about 2 apples)

Yields 18 muffins

Apple Quinoa Oatmeal Muffins

COOKING WITH MICHELE   ❧   MICHELE MORRIS

About 60 percent of the nation's production of apples comes from Washington, including just about every variety imaginable. These nutritious muffins are a perfect way to use up any apples that are starting to get soft.

Preheat the oven to 375 degrees. Line the muffin tins with 18 paper liners and spray the liners with cooking spray.

Combine the quinoa and water in a small saucepan and bring to a boil. Cover, reduce the heat, and cook until fluffy and the water has evaporated, about 15 minutes. Pour the quinoa into a bowl to cool.

Place 1 cup of the oats in a food processor and process until the oats are finely ground. Add the oats to a medium bowl, along with the whole wheat flour, baking soda, baking powder, cinnamon, and salt. Stir together and set aside.

Add the sugar and canola oil to a mixing bowl and mix on medium speed until combined; add the eggs 1 at a time, mixing until incorporated. Add the yogurt and mix until smooth.

Combine the cooked quinoa with the dry ingredients and add to the sugar and eggs; mix on low until incorporated. Fold in the remaining oats and the diced apples, and stir to make sure everything is combined.

Portion the batter into the prepared muffin tins and bake until a toothpick inserted into the center comes out clean, about 15 minutes.

Tart shell

½ cup (1 stick) unsalted butter, cut into pieces

4 teaspoons olive oil

4 tablespoons water

4 teaspoons sugar

⅛ teaspoon salt

1⅓ cups flour

Quiche filling

2 eggs

2 egg yolks

2 cups heavy cream or half-and-half

2 tablespoons extra virgin olive oil

1 sweet onion, diced

1 tablespoon butter

1 tablespoon minced fresh garlic

1 tablespoon minced fresh shallot

¼ cup white wine

1 cup grilled and diced summer squash (about 1 small squash)

1 cup grilled and roughly chopped artichoke hearts
(see Note on page 6)

1 teaspoon chopped fresh parsley

1 teaspoon chopped fresh thyme

1 teaspoon chopped fresh rosemary

9 ounces grated Gruyère cheese (about 2½ cups)

Salt and pepper

Serves 8

Artichoke and Summer Squash Quiche with Gruyère Cheese

THE MARC, THE MARCUS WHITMAN HOTEL, WALLA WALLA
EXECUTIVE CHEF ANTONIO CAMPOLIO

The Marc at the Marcus Whitman Hotel, a favorite among visitors to the Walla Walla wine country, features seasonal food like this quiche in a casual yet elegant setting.

For the tart shell:
Preheat the oven to 400 degrees.

Combine the butter, oil, water, sugar, and salt in a medium oven-safe bowl. Place the bowl in the oven until the butter is bubbling and starts to brown just around the edges, about 15 minutes. Remove the bowl from the oven and add the flour all at once, stirring it in quickly until it comes together and forms a ball that pulls away from the sides of the bowl. Transfer the dough to an 11-inch nonstick tart pan with a removable bottom and spread it a bit with a spatula.

Once the dough is cool enough to handle, press it to evenly cover the bottom and up the sides of the tart mold, making sure there are no cracks in the dough. Prick the dough all over with the tines of a fork and bake the tart shell for 6 minutes. Remove the tart shell from the oven and set it aside to cool in the tart pan.

For the quiche filling:
Combine the eggs, egg yolks, and cream in a medium bowl, whisk together, and set aside.

Heat a medium sauté pan over medium heat and add the olive oil. When the oil is hot, add the onions and sauté until translucent, about 5 minutes. Add the butter and melt, and then add the garlic and shallot and sauté for another minute. Add the white wine and simmer for another minute.

(continued on page 6)

Remove from the stove and transfer the mixture to a bowl. Add the squash, artichoke hearts, parsley, thyme, and rosemary to the mixture and let the mixture cool slightly. Add 2 cups of the Gruyère cheese to the mixture and season with salt and pepper to taste.

To assemble:
Preheat the oven to 350 degrees.

Place the tart on a baking sheet and spoon the vegetable mixture into the bottom of the tart shell. Pour the egg and cream mixture over the top of the vegetables. Place the tart in the oven and bake until the center is almost set, about 45 to 50 minutes, rotating the pan once or twice to ensure even cooking.

Sprinkle the remaining cheese on top and bake for an additional 5 minutes. Let cool at room temperature for 5 to 10 minutes before removing the tart from the tart pan and serving.

✤ *Note: If you don't have time to trim fresh artichokes down to the hearts, use canned artichoke hearts instead and skip the grilling. You may also use a pre-prepared pie crust.*

Biscuits

5 cups flour

2 tablespoons sugar

1 teaspoon baking soda

1 teaspoon baking powder

1 teaspoon kosher salt

1½ cups (3 sticks) cold butter, diced

8 ounces chopped dates
(about 2 cups)

½ pound bacon, cooked
and crumbled

1 cup cold buttermilk

1 tablespoon maple extract

Melted butter

Maple glaze

1 cup powdered sugar, sifted

¼ cup maple syrup

Water, as needed

Yields 24 biscuits

Bacon Maple Date Biscuits with Maple Glaze

THE WANDERING GOOSE, SEATTLE
OWNER AND BAKER HEATHER L. EARNHARDT

The maple glaze combined with the bacon and dates in these biscuits creates a flaky version of a decadent cinnamon roll. They are easy to make, freeze well, and you might find it hard to limit yourself to just one.

For the biscuits:
Preheat the oven to 400 degrees.

Combine the flour, sugar, baking soda, baking powder, and salt in mixing bowl and mix on low. Add the butter and mix on low until the butter is the size of small peas, about 5 minutes. Add the dates and bacon, and with the mixer running on low, add the buttermilk and maple extract. Mix only until just blended, taking care not to over mix. The dough will be somewhat dry and crumbly.

Place the dough onto a lightly floured surface, pat gently into a 1-inch-thick round, and cut using a 2½-inch biscuit cutter dipped in flour (*see Note*). Set the biscuits on a baking sheet and brush the biscuits with melted butter. Bake until lightly browned, about 15 to 20 minutes, rotating the pans halfway through.

For the maple glaze:
Combine the powdered sugar and syrup and mix until smooth. If the glaze is too thick, thin with a few drops of water. Drizzle over the cooled biscuits and serve.

❧ **Note:** *Do not twist the cutter when cutting the biscuits as this will seal the sides and the biscuits will not rise as high. As you cut the biscuits, gather up the scraps of dough and reshape into a disk to continue cutting into biscuits until all of the dough is used.*

Blueberry sauce

1⅓ cups water

1⅓ cups sugar

3 tablespoons cornstarch

3 cups blueberries, divided

1 tablespoon butter

Morning glories

1 large loaf French bread, diced

¼ cup maple syrup

2 cups milk

1 cup half-and-half

2 tablespoons vanilla extract

½ teaspoon ground cinnamon

¼ teaspoon ground nutmeg

12 eggs

1 (8-ounce) package cream cheese,
    softened

¼ cup brown sugar

1 small lemon, zested

3 cups blueberries

Serves 12

❧ *Note: You may prepare the morning
glories in a variety of baking dishes:
twelve 6-ounce ramekins, two 8-inch
round or square casserole dishes, or
one 13 x 9 x 2-inch dish.*

Blueberry Morning Glories with Warm Blueberry Sauce

RUN OF THE RIVER INN & REFUGE, LEAVENWORTH
INNKEEPER JANNA BOLLINGER

*Run of the River is surrounded by a designated bird refuge that is home
to deer, coyote, and the occasional bear and elk, making it the perfect
location for a romantic getaway.*

For the blueberry sauce:

Combine the water, sugar, cornstarch, and 2 cups of the blueberries
in a medium saucepan and simmer until thick, about 5 minutes. Stir
in the remaining blueberries and the butter and refrigerate until ready
to use. To serve, reheat briefly in the microwave.

For the morning glories:

Place the bread in a large bowl. Combine the maple syrup, milk,
half-and-half, vanilla, cinnamon, nutmeg, and eggs in a large bowl
and whisk until well blended. Pour the egg mixture over the bread,
cover, and refrigerate overnight.

Preheat the oven to 350 degrees. Spray the bottom of a 13 x 9 x
2-inch casserole dish (*see Note*) with cooking spray. Combine the
cream cheese, brown sugar, and lemon zest in a small bowl, stir
to combine, and set aside.

Stir the bread and egg mixture to ensure it's evenly mixed, then pour
half of the bread and egg mixture into the casserole dish. Layer the
blueberries on top of the bread, and then place small dollops of the
cream cheese mixture evenly across the blueberries. Top the casserole
with the remaining bread and egg mixture.

Place the casserole on a baking sheet, spray a piece of aluminum
foil so it won't stick to the bread, and cover the casserole. Bake for
30 minutes, and then remove the foil and finish baking until golden
brown and completely set, about 15 minutes more. Serve with warm
blueberry sauce.

Béchamel sauce

2 tablespoons extra virgin olive oil
or melted butter

2 tablespoons flour

1 ½ cups milk, warmed *(see Note)*

Pinch nutmeg

Salt

Bouchons

2 tablespoons flour

2 tablespoons cornstarch

½ teaspoon baking powder

¼ teaspoon salt

4 large eggs, at room temperature,
separated

¼ cup milk

1 tablespoon chopped fresh herbs,
or 1 teaspoon dried

¾ cup grated cheddar cheese

½ cup grated Parmesan cheese,
for garnish

Minced fresh chives, for garnish

Serves 6

Bouchons Baked
with Béchamel Sauce

WILLCOX HOUSE COUNTRY INN, SEABECK, THE KITSAP PENINSULA
INNKEEPER CECELIA HUGHES

*These easy soufflés can be made ahead of time and refrigerated for a couple
of days and then baked with the béchamel sauce when ready to serve. For
variety, place a slice of Canadian bacon under the soufflés before baking.*

For the béchamel sauce:
Heat the olive oil in a small saucepan over medium-high heat, add
the flour, and whisk until it bubbles. While whisking, slowly add the
warmed milk to the roux and continue whisking until the mixture
begins to boil and thickens. Season with nutmeg and salt to taste.

For the bouchons:
Preheat the oven to 350 degrees. Spray six 5-ounce ramekins
or custard cups with cooking spray and set aside. Sift the flour,
cornstarch, baking powder, and salt together and set aside.

Beat the egg yolks in a medium bowl and whisk in the milk. Stir
the herbs and cheddar cheese into the yolk mixture. Add the egg
whites to a mixing bowl and beat to form soft peaks.

Whisk the dry ingredients into the egg yolk mixture until smooth,
and then fold in the egg whites, taking care not to deflate the whites.
Divide the batter among the custard dishes and set the dishes on
a baking sheet. Bake until set, about 15 to 18 minutes.

Cool for about 5 minutes, and then carefully unmold the soufflés
and place them on a parchment paper-lined baking sheet. Pour
about ¼ cup of the béchamel over each soufflé and sprinkle the
Parmesan cheese evenly over the soufflés. Bake until lightly browned
and bubbling, about 15 minutes. Remove from the oven and garnish
with chives before serving.

❧ ***Note:*** *At the inn, Cecelia Hughes uses 2% milk in both the béchamel sauce
and the soufflés, but you may also use 1% or whole milk if desired.*

Cinnamon Pear Pancakes

CHINABERRY HILL, TACOMA ❧ INNKEEPER CECIL WAYMAN

This unusual presentation for pancakes always draws "oohs and ahs" from guests when they are brought to the table at Chinaberry Hill, an eclectic bed-and-breakfast set in a grand Victorian house.

1 large pear

Ground cinnamon

¼ cup maple syrup,
    plus more for serving

¾ cup flour

1 teaspoon baking soda

½ teaspoon salt

3 tablespoons melted butter

1 egg, lightly beaten

1 cup buttermilk

Butter

Sour cream, for garnish

Cinnamon, for garnish

Serves 2 to 3 (6 pancakes)

Working from the center of the whole pear, cut 6 uniformly flat slices, each about ¼ inch thick. Carefully cut out any pieces of the core or seeds from the slices, leaving the pear slices intact. Discard any leftover "ends." Lay the slices flat on a large cutting board, dust with cinnamon, and drizzle with the maple syrup.

Combine the flour, baking soda, and salt in a large bowl and whisk thoroughly. Add the butter, egg, and buttermilk and whisk, leaving some of the lumps in the mixture.

Heat a griddle to 325 degrees or a large, nonstick skillet pan over medium–high heat. Butter the griddle or pan generously and place the pear slices (cinnamon side down) on the griddle, allowing them to cook for 1 minute. Using a ¼-cup measure, pour the pancake mix onto the center of each slice, making sure the batter covers the pear completely. When the bubbles that surface on the pancakes remain open and the edges are set (about 3 to 4 minutes), turn the pancake with a wide spatula and finish cooking for 1 to 2 minutes on the second side.

Serve the pancakes with a dollop of sour cream, a sprinkling of ground cinnamon, and maple syrup.

8 cups frozen shredded
   hash brown potatoes,
   cooked until golden brown

8 hard-boiled eggs, peeled

1 cup (2 sticks) butter,
   melted and divided

1 teaspoon dry mustard

Pinch cayenne pepper

Pinch paprika

2 teaspoons grated onion

Salt and pepper

2 cups sour cream, plus more
   for garnish

2 tablespoons grated
   Parmesan cheese

1 cup breadcrumbs

1 tablespoon chopped parsley

Serves 8

Eggs Caprice

ABENDBLUME, LEAVENWORTH   &   INNKEEPER RENEE SEXAUER

*Although the Abendblume inn is set just a mile from downtown
Leavenworth, its location in the Cascades along with the hand-carved
wood ceilings, iron railings, and extensive stonework will leave you
feeling as if you've escaped to a retreat in the Old World.*

Preheat the oven to 350 degrees. Spray a 13 x 9 x 2-inch baking dish
with cooking spray and spread the cooked hash browns evenly in
the bottom of the baking dish.

Cut the eggs in half lengthwise, remove the yolks, and combine the
yolks with ½ cup of the melted butter, mustard, cayenne, paprika,
and onion; season with salt and pepper to taste. Fill the egg halves
with the yolk mixture, using up the entire filling.

Place the egg halves, yoke side down, on top of the cooked hash
browns. Use a squeeze bottle to drizzle the sour cream over the
eggs, and then sprinkle the Parmesan cheese over the top.

Brown the breadcrumbs in a small skillet using the remaining melted
butter. Sprinkle the breadcrumbs and chopped parsley over the top
and bake for 20 minutes. Serve warm with additional sour cream
for garnish.

1 cup oats

4 teaspoons brown sugar

¼ teaspoon cinnamon

Pinch salt

½ cup diced apples (see Note)

½ cup dried cranberries

1 cup almond milk (see Note)

½ teaspoon vanilla

2 teaspoons butter (omit for vegan)

Whipped cream, for garnish
    (omit for vegan)

Nutmeg, for garnish (optional)

Serves 2

Fruit and Oats Breakfast Pudding

SWANTOWN INN, OLYMPIA
INNKEEPERS NATHAN AND CASEY ALLAN

Innkeeper Casey Allan knows how important it is to meet the dietary needs of all of her guests, so she offers this gluten-free, dairy-free, vegan recipe that suits a myriad of diets while still pleasing everyone. As a bonus, kids love it too.

Preheat the oven to 350 degrees. Spray two 10-ounce ramekins with cooking spray.

Combine the oats, brown sugar, cinnamon, salt, and fruit in a small bowl and mix well. Pour into the prepared ramekins.

Combine the almond milk and vanilla and then pour into the ramekins. Top each with a teaspoon of butter broken into small pieces to dot the top. Bake the ramekins until completely set, about 30 minutes. Serve warm topped with whipped cream and nutmeg.

❧ **Note:** *For variety, replace the apples and cranberries with peaches, mixed berries, or a combination of bananas and walnuts. Also, if your diet allows dairy, you may substitute milk for the almond milk.*

3 cups pastry flour
    *(see Guidelines for Recipes
    on page xviii)*

4 teaspoons baking powder

¾ cup sugar

¼ teaspoon grated nutmeg

3 eggs

1 cup buttermilk

1 teaspoon vanilla extract

¾ cup canola oil

1½ cups marionberries,
    for garnish

Powdered sugar, for garnish

Serves 6

Marionberry Pancakes

SIX SEVEN RESTAURANT, THE EDGEWATER HOTEL, SEATTLE
EXECUTIVE CHEF JOHN ROBERTS

Chef Roberts calls for adding the marionberries to the batter before cooking the pancakes. It's easier to handle the pancakes if you garnish with the berries instead, as suggested below.

Sift the flour, baking powder, sugar, and nutmeg together in a medium bowl. In a separate bowl, beat together the eggs, buttermilk, vanilla, and oil. Mix in the dry ingredients.

Preheat a nonstick electric griddle to 325 degrees or heat a nonstick pan over medium-high heat. Portion pancakes onto the griddle using a ¼-cup measuring cup and cook until golden brown, about 2 to 3 minutes per side.

Garnish with marionberries and powdered sugar and serve with your favorite syrup.

2 tablespoons butter

4 ounces smoked salmon, flaked

2 ounces Dungeness crab

½ teaspoon chopped fresh dill

2 cups baby spinach,
    stems removed

6 eggs, whipped until light
    in color

Pepper

Sour cream, for garnish

Minced chives, for garnish

Serves 2 to 3

Northwest Scrambled Eggs

BONNEVILLE HOT SPRINGS RESORT AND SPA, NORTH BONNEVILLE
EXECUTIVE CHEF EDWARD J. TIPPEL III

*Bonneville Hot Springs Resort and Spa is situated in the beautiful
Columbia River Gorge, just down the road from Multnomah Falls.
The salmon and crab bring a salty flavor to the eggs in this scramble,
so there is no need for additional salt.*

Heat a nonstick skillet over medium heat and melt the butter in
the pan. Add the salmon, crab, and dill and sauté until just warmed
through, about 1 minute. Add the spinach and cook until wilted. Add
the eggs and cook just until the eggs are softly cooked. Season with
pepper to taste and top with sour cream and minced chives to serve.

1 large navel orange, zested

4 teaspoons orange oil

1 tablespoon vanilla extract

⅓ cup honey

6 eggs

¾ cup heavy cream

¾ cup orange juice

2 tablespoons butter

6 large croissants,
    sliced in half horizontally

Maple syrup

Powdered sugar, for garnish

6 orange slices, for garnish

Serves 6

Orange Butter Croissant French Toast

CHINABERRY HILL, TACOMA ❧ INNKEEPER CECIL WAYMAN

Returning guests at Chinaberry Hill probably request this recipe more than any other. Originally brought to the inn by an employee, over the years sources of orange flavor have been added to the recipe to intensify the "orange experience."

Combine the orange zest, orange oil, vanilla, honey, and eggs in a large bowl and beat thoroughly with a whisk until the honey is completely dissolved. Add the cream and orange juice and whisk until the batter is well mixed.

Preheat a griddle or large sauté pan over medium heat and melt the butter on the surface. Dip the croissants into the egg mixture and place them on the griddle, cut side up. Turn after about 3 to 4 minutes and continue to cook on the cut side until nicely golden brown, about 2 to 3 more minutes. Place the French toast on individual plates or a serving platter, drizzle with maple syrup, dust with powdered sugar, and garnish with twisted orange slices.

1 cup water

1 cup chardonnay wine

½ cup sugar

3 cinnamon sticks

8 oranges, peeled
    and sliced horizontally

Serves 8

Oranges Chardonnay

THE INN ON ORCAS ISLAND, DEER HARBOR, ORCAS ISLAND
INNKEEPER JEREMY TRUMBLE

Set in sunny Deer Harbor, The Inn on Orcas Island has been called one of the best seaside getaways. The inn's simple orange breakfast side dish is surprisingly complex in flavor and could also be served as a light dessert.

Combine the water, wine, sugar, and cinnamon in a medium saucepan over medium-high heat and bring to a boil. Cover, reduce the heat, and simmer for 10 minutes. Place the sliced oranges in a large bowl and pour the chardonnay mixture over the oranges. Refrigerate for 4 hours before serving.

2 pounds russet potatoes,
    diced into 1-inch cubes

Extra virgin olive oil, for frying

1 tablespoon minced fresh rosemary

1 teaspoon sea salt

Serves 4 to 6

Roasted Rosemary Brunch Potatoes

LUNA, SPOKANE   ☎   EXECUTIVE CHEF ZACH STONE

The addition of rosemary and sea salt transforms the simple breakfast potato to something special at Luna, Spokane's top-rated restaurant.

Place potatoes in a medium stockpot, cover with water, and bring to a boil. Cook the potatoes until soft, about 20 minutes, and then drain.

Heat a large skillet over medium–high heat and add enough olive oil to coat the bottom of the pan to a depth of ¼ inch. Fry the potatoes until crispy and browned, about 20 to 30 minutes. Remove the pan from the heat and toss the hot potatoes with the rosemary and sea salt before serving.

3 ounces Italian sausage,
   cooked and crumbled

3 ounces fresh baby spinach
   (about 2 cups)

1 green onion, chopped

½ cup grated cheddar cheese

½ cup grated Swiss cheese

4 ounces cream cheese,
   cut into small cubes

8 eggs

½ cup half-and-half

½ teaspoon dried basil

½ teaspoon garlic salt

½ teaspoon Italian seasoning
   or dried oregano

Serves 6 to 8

Sausage Spinach Frittata

ABENDBLUME, LEAVENWORTH   &   INNKEEPER RENEE SEXAUER

If you're trying to save time in the morning, this cheesy frittata may be partially prepared the night before.

Preheat the oven to 350 degrees. Grease a 9-inch quiche dish with butter, or spray with cooking spray.

Layer the sausage in the prepared quiche dish and then top, in order, with the spinach, green onion, cheddar cheese, Swiss cheese, and cream cheese. At this point, the frittata may be covered and refrigerated overnight.

Combine the eggs and half-and-half in a medium bowl and add the basil, garlic salt, and Italian seasoning. Beat the egg mixture and pour over the ingredients in the quiche dish. Bake until the eggs are just set, about 25 to 30 minutes, taking care not to over-bake. Let stand for a few minutes before slicing and serving.

Swantown Scones

SWANTOWN INN, OLYMPIA
INNKEEPERS NATHAN AND CASEY ALLAN

The Swantown Inn, located in a quiet neighborhood of Olympia in an 1887 Queen Anne/Eastlake Victorian mansion, is listed on both the city and state historical registers. Innkeeper Casey Allan says her scones are by far the most popular of the various baked goods served there, and during seven years of running the inn, she estimates they've made over 24,000 scones.

Preheat the oven to 450 degrees.

Stir together the flour, sugar, baking soda, and salt in a medium bowl. Use your fingers or a pastry cutter to blend the butter into the flour until the mixture is crumbly. Make a well in the center of the mixture and gradually add the buttermilk, stirring gently with a fork. Stir in the fruit and nuts and mix just until a soft dough is formed.

Turn the dough out onto a lightly floured surface, pat into a circle ½ inch thick at the edge with a slightly thicker center, and cut into 8 triangular pieces. Place the pieces on a baking stone or an ungreased baking sheet and bake until golden brown, about 12 minutes. The scones are best served warm.

❧ *Note: Casey recommends adding any of these combinations of fruit and nuts to the dough: dried cranberries and walnuts, dried blueberries (to avoid purple scones, do not use fresh or frozen blueberries), raisins tossed with ¼ teaspoon cinnamon, or half a ripe banana (reduce buttermilk to ½ cup) and walnuts.*

2 cups flour, sifted

2 tablespoons sugar

½ teaspoon baking soda

½ teaspoon salt

4 tablespoons cold unsalted butter, cut into cubes

¾ cup plus 2 tablespoons buttermilk

½ cup fruit and nuts of your choice (see Note)

Yields 8 scones

8 eggs

½ cup sugar

1 cup flour

1 cup milk

1 teaspoon baking powder

1 teaspoon salt

1½ teaspoons vanilla extract

4 tablespoons butter, melted

Butter, for garnish

Powdered sugar, for garnish

3 to 4 cups fresh fruit
(chopped mixed fruit or berries)

Serves 8 (16 pancakes)

Swedish Pancakes

THE GREENLAKE GUEST HOUSE, SEATTLE
INNKEEPERS BLAYNE AND JULIE MCAFERTY

Perched across the street from Seattle's beloved Green Lake Park, the Greenlake Guest House is an oasis in North Seattle. These pancakes, similar to a French crêpe, are a staple on their gourmet breakfast menu.

Blend the eggs, sugar, flour, and milk in a blender on low speed until combined, about 30 seconds. With the blender running, add the baking powder, salt, vanilla, and melted butter.

Spray an 8-inch nonstick round frying pan with cooking spray and heat over medium-high heat. Add ¼ cup of batter to the hot pan, tilting the pan so that the batter covers the pan evenly, and cook on the first side until set, about 3 minutes. Flip the pancake and finish cooking on the second side, about 1 minute more.

Remove the pancake from the pan, spread with butter and sifted powdered sugar, and roll up. Repeat with the remaining pancake batter. To serve, spoon fresh fruit over the top, garnish with powdered sugar, and serve warm.

1 cup chopped walnuts

3 cups oats

½ cup unsweetened flaked coconut

½ cup slivered almonds

½ cup roughly chopped pecans

¼ cup sesame seeds

1 teaspoon cinnamon

1 teaspoon vanilla extract

¼ cup Steen's Cane Syrup
    or maple syrup
    (see Sources on page 174)

¼ cup honey

6 tablespoons canola oil

1 ½ tablespoons dark brown sugar

½ cup dried sour cherries
    or chopped apricots

1 cup raisins

¼ cup currants or dried blueberries

Yields 8 cups

The Wandering Goose Granola

THE WANDERING GOOSE, SEATTLE
OWNER AND BAKER HEATHER L. EARNHARDT

While many know Earnhardt for her outstanding baking skills, the restaurateur is also a writer of children's literature, including The Wandering Goose: A Modern Fable of How Love Goes *and* Bug and Goose.

Preheat the oven to 325 degrees. Spray a rimmed baking sheet with cooking spray and set aside.

Combine the walnuts, oats, coconut, almonds, pecans, and sesame seeds in a large bowl and set aside. Combine the cinnamon, vanilla, syrup, honey, oil, and brown sugar in a saucepan and heat over medium heat until the sugar is dissolved and the mixture begins to simmer. Pour the mixture over the dry ingredients and mix with a rubber spatula.

Spoon the granola onto the baking sheet and cook until browned and crispy, about 25 minutes, stirring the mixture several times and taking care not to burn the granola. Remove from the oven and cool to room temperature. Add the dried fruit and mix together. Serve in bowls with milk or yogurt. Store extra granola in a covered container.

2 cups frozen shredded
    hash brown potatoes,
    cooked until golden brown

1 teaspoon fajita seasoning

½ teaspoon cumin

2 cups shredded sharp cheddar
    cheese

½ pound ground Italian sausage,
    cooked and crumbled

4 green onions, sliced

2 (4-ounce) cans chopped
    green chiles, drained

1 cup sliced black olives

1 cup corn kernels (fresh or frozen)

1 small zucchini, diced

1 red bell pepper, diced

½ cup chopped cilantro

2 cups shredded pepper
    jack cheese or Mexican
    4-cheese blend

1 (14-ounce) can black beans,
    drained and rinsed

20 eggs

1 cup heavy cream

½ cup half-and-half

Cilantro sprigs, for garnish

Sour cream, for garnish

Salsa, for garnish

Serves 12 to 16

Wild Iris Inn Fiesta Frittata

THE WILD IRIS INN, LA CONNER
INNKEEPER AND OWNER LORI FARNELL

This casserole may be made the night before and refrigerated until you're ready to bake it. At the inn, they serve the frittata with sour cream and a selection of salsas.

Preheat the oven to 350 degrees. Spray a 13 x 9 x 2-inch baking dish with cooking spray.

Spread the cooked hash browns on the bottom of the baking dish and sprinkle with the fajita seasoning and cumin. In order, layer the cheddar cheese, sausage, green onions, chiles, olives, corn, zucchini, red pepper, cilantro, jack cheese, and black beans over the top.

Set the casserole on a baking sheet. Whisk the eggs, cream, and half-and-half together in a large bowl and then pour over the casserole. Bake until the center is firm, about 1 hour.

Let the frittata stand for a few minutes at room temperature before slicing. Garnish slices of the frittata with cilantro and serve with sour cream and salsa.

¼ cup roughly chopped walnuts

¼ cup sliced or slivered almonds

¼ cup pine nuts

6 fresh or dried figs,
    cut into quarters

6 large dates, pitted and chopped

½ cup honey

¼ cup water

1 lemon, juiced

1 cinnamon stick

2 cups Greek yogurt

Fresh mint leaves, for garnish

Serves 4

Yogurt with Fig and Date Compote

CHERRY CHALET BED AND BREAKFAST, KENNEWICK
INNKEEPERS STEVE AND RAINY SAUER

Innkeeper Steve Sauer's father, Leonard, planted Sauer's Orchard in 1972. More than forty years later, this second-generation farming family harvests cherries, peaches, and apricots annually. For variety, try adding dried cranberries and raisins to the figs and dates in this easy breakfast recipe, or replace the figs with cherries or apricots.

Toast the nuts in a sauté pan over medium heat just until they become fragrant, and then remove the nuts from the pan and set aside.

Combine the figs, dates, honey, water, lemon juice, and cinnamon stick in a small saucepan over medium heat and cook until the fruit is soft, about 10 minutes. Cool slightly, and then remove the cinnamon stick and discard it.

Divide the yogurt evenly among four individual bowls and spoon the warm fruit onto the yogurt. Sprinkle with nuts and garnish with fresh mint leaves before serving.

Appetizers & Snacks

Barbecue Duck Eggrolls, p. 30

Asparagus

1 bunch large asparagus spears,
  tough ends removed

1 bunch radishes

1 bunch green onions

¼ cup red wine vinegar

1 tablespoon kosher salt

1 shallot, minced

1 tablespoon chopped
  fresh thyme leaves

½ teaspoon pepper

¼ cup canola oil

¼ cup extra virgin olive oil

Crostini

1 small baguette, sliced into
  12 crostini, ends discarded

Extra virgin olive oil

4 ounces fresh chèvre,
  softened at room temperature

1 garlic clove, minced

1 tablespoon chopped fresh herbs
  (basil, tarragon, or oregano)

Grated Parmesan or Asiago
  cheese, for garnish

Serves 12

Asparagus and Chèvre Crostini

CHEF AND WRITER LISA NAKAMURA

Chef Nakamura, who was busy working to open Gnocchi Bar in Seattle when this book went to press, actually served this fresh and savory appetizer at her popular former restaurant, Allium, on Orcas Island. Although the crostini pairs well with many wines, she recommends trying it with a dry cider from Washington State.

For the asparagus:
Peel the asparagus stalks halfway to the top with a vegetable peeler. Bring a large pot filled with salted water to a boil and blanch the asparagus for 4 to 5 minutes. Remove and immediately submerge the asparagus in a bowl of ice water; drain well. Cut the asparagus on the diagonal in thin slices, about ¼ inch thick.

Slice the radishes in thin rounds using either a knife or mandoline. The slices should be almost transparent. Slice the green onions very thinly on the bias. Combine the asparagus, radishes, and green onions in a medium bowl.

Combine the vinegar, salt, shallot, thyme, and pepper in a small bowl and whisk together until the salt is dissolved. Slowly whisk in the canola oil and olive oil. Add enough marinade to just coat the vegetables, and then let sit for an hour at room temperature for the flavors to meld.

For the crostini:

Preheat the oven to 350 degrees. Brush the baguette slices lightly with olive oil and toast in the oven until golden and crisp, about 10 minutes; let cool. Crostini can be made several days ahead, cooled, and stored in an airtight container.

Mix the chèvre with the garlic and fresh herbs. Spread each crostini with the soft chèvre mixture. Place some of the marinated asparagus mixture on top. Finish with a sprinkling of grated cheese and serve.

Rhubarb barbecue sauce

(see Note on page 31)

2 pounds rhubarb stalks, diced

1 sweet onion, diced

1 tablespoon sliced garlic

1 tablespoon extra virgin olive oil

1 (28-ounce) can tomato sauce

1 teaspoon ground cinnamon

½ cup port wine

¼ cup red wine vinegar

1 tablespoon Dijon mustard

1 cup sugar

½ cup honey

1 tablespoon salt

Spinach puree

1 pound baby spinach

2 tablespoons water

½ bunch Italian parsley

2 ounces fresh basil leaves

1 tablespoon chopped garlic

1 lemon, juiced

¼ cup extra virgin olive oil

Pinch salt

Barbecue Duck Eggrolls

CAFE NOLA, BAINBRIDGE ISLAND
CHEF AND OWNER KEVIN WARREN

While the crunchy texture of these flavorful eggrolls is enticing, you may cut calories and skip a step by rolling the filling in softened spring roll wrappers (rice paper) instead of eggroll wrappers and eating them fresh instead of fried.

For the rhubarb barbecue sauce:
Combine the rhubarb, onion, garlic, olive oil, tomato sauce, cinnamon, port, vinegar, mustard, sugar, honey, and salt in a medium saucepan and bring to a simmer. Cover and simmer over low heat until all of the ingredients have broken down, about 30 minutes. Let cool slightly and then puree in a food processor or blender.

For the spinach puree:
Add the spinach and water to a large pot and cover. Set over high heat and steam the spinach until it is completely cooked down, about 3 minutes. Strain the spinach and discard the liquid. Transfer the spinach to a food processor; add the parsley, basil, garlic, lemon juice, olive oil, and salt and puree until smooth and the consistency of a loose pesto sauce.

Lemon yogurt

1 lemon, zested

1 cup plain yogurt

Eggrolls

Meat from 3 confit duck legs
(about 1½ cups)
(see Sources on page 174)

4 green onions, thinly sliced

2 small carrots, grated

½ head green cabbage,
thinly sliced

1 jalapeño, seeded and minced

1 red bell pepper, finely chopped

2 tablespoons minced
pickled ginger

1 teaspoon pickled ginger juice

½ cup chopped cilantro

½ cup chopped parsley

¼ cup chopped mint

2 limes, juiced

1 cup chopped cooked
rice noodles (see Note)

16 to 18 eggroll wrappers

Canola oil, for frying

Yields 16 to 18 eggrolls

For the lemon yogurt:
Stir the lemon zest into the yogurt and store in the refrigerator until ready to use.

For the eggrolls:
Allow the prepared duck confit to sit at room temperature for 1 hour and pick through to remove any bones or tendons. Shred the meat into small pieces and fold in ½ cup of the rhubarb barbecue sauce. Add the green onions, carrots, cabbage, jalapeño, bell pepper, ginger, juice, cilantro, parsley, mint, lime juice, and cooked rice noodles and stir gently to combine well.

Place an eggroll wrapper on a flat surface with a corner pointing toward you. Place ⅓ cup of the filling on the front half of the eggroll wrapper. Fold the point over the filling and then fold the sides in like an envelope. Wet the point of the wrapper that is away from you and continue rolling up completely, pressing the wet point to seal the eggroll. Set aside and repeat with the remaining eggroll wrappers.

Add canola oil to a depth of 3 inches in a saucepan and heat over medium-high heat. Fry the eggrolls two at a time until lightly browned on both sides, and then drain on paper towels. Repeat until all of the eggrolls are cooked.

To assemble:
Swipe a generous dollop of lemon yogurt and a squiggle of spinach puree on appetizer plates. Cut the cooked eggrolls in half and place on the plates, and then serve with more of the barbecue sauce for dipping.

❧ **Note:** *You may use another ready-made barbecue sauce of your choice if you don't have the time or ingredients to make the rhubarb barbecue sauce in this recipe. To cook rice noodles, pour 4 to 5 cups of boiling water over 1 cup of dry rice noodles and let the noodles sit for 15 minutes. Strain and cool the noodles, then roughly chop.*

4¾ cups flour

⅓ cup sugar

4½ teaspoons baking powder

12 ounces lager-style beer

Butter, for serving

Sea salt, for serving

Serves 8 to 12

Beer Bread

BLIND PIG BISTRO, SEATTLE & CHEF CHARLES WALPOLE

Chef Walpole was previously a chef at the well-known Anchovies & Olives before launching his own restaurant, Blind Pig Bistro. He uses Hales Ales Kolsch for this simple bread and makes it in small loaves to serve diners. Since the bread is made without salt, be sure to serve it with plenty of butter and some high-quality, flaky sea salt.

Preheat the oven to 350 degrees. Grease a 9 x 5 x 4–inch loaf pan.

Mix the flour, sugar, and baking powder in a medium bowl. Add the beer and mix until the dry ingredients are fully moistened. Turn the dough out onto a lightly floured board and knead just until smooth, about 1 minute.

Shape the dough into a log and place it in the loaf pan. Bake for 30 minutes and then, if desired, broil for 1 minute to brown the top. Rest the bread for 10 minutes before removing it from the loaf pan and slicing.

Tzatziki sauce

1 cucumber, peeled and seeded

2 cups plain yogurt

1½ teaspoons minced garlic

1 tablespoon apple cider vinegar

1½ teaspoons lemon juice

1 tablespoon roughly
    chopped fresh mint

½ teaspoon kosher salt

2 tablespoons extra virgin olive oil

Chickpea cakes

1 cucumber, peeled, seeded,
    and shredded

Kosher salt

2 (15-ounce) cans chickpeas,
    drained and rinsed

3 eggs, lightly beaten

3 tablespoons extra virgin olive oil

1½ teaspoons garam masala

¼ teaspoon cayenne pepper

½ cup plain Greek yogurt, divided

⅓ cup thinly sliced green onions

⅓ cup chopped cilantro

⅓ cup minced roasted
    red bell pepper

(continued on page 34)

Chickpea Cakes with Tzatziki Sauce

KEENAN'S AT THE PIER, THE CHRYSALIS INN AND SPA, BELLINGHAM
EXECUTIVE CHEF ROB HOLMES

You can freeze any extra chickpea cakes before cooking them. Lay the panko-coated cakes in a single layer and freeze completely before transferring to a plastic bag for storage. When you are ready to use them, simply thaw in the refrigerator and bring to room temperature before frying the cakes. Chef Holmes suggests serving these cakes as a vegetarian alternative to a burger.

For the tzatziki sauce:
Place the cucumber in the food processor and pulse until chopped. Transfer to a strainer and press out as much excess liquid from the cucumber as possible.

Combine ½ cup of the yogurt with the cucumber, garlic, vinegar, lemon juice, mint, and salt in the food processor and blend until the solids are finely minced and the liquid is smooth, about 1 minute. While the food processor is running, add the olive oil to the mixture. Transfer the mixture to a large bowl and whisk in the remaining 1½ cups of yogurt until combined. Refrigerate until ready to use.

For the chickpea cakes:
Toss the shredded cucumber with ½ teaspoon of kosher salt in a strainer and set aside to drain.

Place the chickpeas in a food processor and pulse to coarsely chop. Combine the eggs, olive oil, garam masala, cayenne, and ⅛ teaspoon of kosher salt in a medium bowl and whisk together. Add the chickpeas, yogurt, green onions, cilantro, red pepper, shallot, pepper, and the drained cucumber and mix with a fork to combine the ingredients.

(continued on page 34)

1 heaping tablespoon
    minced shallot

½ teaspoon pepper

3 cups panko breadcrumbs,
    divided

Extra virgin olive oil,
    for cooking chickpea cakes

Yields 18 cakes

Add half of the panko to the chickpea mixture and stir with a rubber spatula until just combined. Adjust salt and pepper to taste.

Use a ¼-cup measuring cup to portion the chickpea mixture onto a baking sheet or cutting board. Press lightly to form 1-inch-thick round chickpea cakes. Pour the remaining panko into a shallow bowl and coat the chickpea cakes with the panko.

Preheat the oven to 200 degrees. Heat a large, heavy-bottomed sauté pan over medium-high heat and add about ½ inch of olive oil. When the oil is hot, add a few chickpea cakes, making sure not to crowd the pan. Cook until golden brown on one side, about 3 minutes. Turn and continue to cook until brown on the other side, about 3 more minutes. Place the cooked chickpea cakes on a baking sheet and hold in the oven to keep warm while you finish cooking the remaining chickpea cakes.

When all of the chickpea cakes have been cooked, place them on a platter and drizzle with tzatziki sauce; serve warm.

Tomato coulis

4 Roma tomatoes, halved lengthwise

1 tablespoon chile oil

½ teaspoon red chili flakes

½ teaspoon salt

¼ teaspoon pepper

1 tablespoon extra virgin olive oil

1 small fennel bulb, diced

1 white onion, diced

4 whole garlic cloves

1 leek, cleaned and chopped, whites only

¼ cup white wine vinegar

½ cup white wine

1 (28-ounce) can plum tomatoes, including juice

2 bay leaves

1 tablespoon fresh thyme leaves, or 1 teaspoon dried

Clams

1 tablespoon canola oil

½ pound fresh pork chorizo sausage

2 to 3 pounds clams

⅔ cup white wine

Extra virgin olive oil

Salt and pepper

Thinly sliced basil, for garnish

Serves 2 to 4

Clams and Chorizo

PRIMA BISTRO, LANGLEY, WHIDBEY ISLAND
CHEF AND OWNER SIEB JURRIAANS

Situated on the South End of Whidbey Island, Prima Bistro offers an incredible view over Saratoga Passage that you can enjoy from the outside deck in good weather. This recipe will make more tomato coulis than needed; the extra may be used for dipping bread or as a pasta sauce and may be frozen.

For the tomato coulis:

Preheat the oven to 400 degrees. Toss the Roma tomatoes with the chile oil, chili flakes, salt, and pepper and lay the tomato halves, face up, on a baking sheet. Roast the tomatoes until their liquids reduce and they caramelize a bit, about 30 minutes.

Heat the olive oil in a large skillet over medium–high heat and cook the fennel, onion, garlic, and leek until they are softened and lightly caramelized. Add the roasted tomatoes and vinegar and simmer together, uncovered, until almost dry. Add the wine and simmer until almost dry as well. Add the canned tomatoes with their juice, bay leaves, and thyme and simmer for 30 minutes. Remove the bay leaves, puree the mixture, and set aside. At Prima Bistro, the chef strains the pureed tomato coulis for a velvety smooth texture, but you may omit this step if desired.

For the clams:

Heat a large skillet over high heat and add the canola oil. When the oil is hot, add the chorizo, using a wooden spoon to break it up. Cook the chorizo partially, and then add the clams, ½ cup of the tomato coulis, and wine. Cover and cook until the clams open, about 8 to 10 minutes.

To serve, ladle the clams into a large serving bowl, discarding any that have not opened. Drizzle with extra virgin olive oil, season with salt and pepper, and garnish with basil.

1 tablespoon extra virgin olive oil

¼ cup diced red bell peppers

¼ cup diced yellow onions

1 (8-ounce) package cream cheese, softened

1 (5.2-ounce) package Boursin® garlic and herb cheese, softened

1 heaping tablespoon finely chopped fresh parsley

½ teaspoon kosher salt

Pinch coarsely ground black pepper

⅛ teaspoon garlic powder

⅛ teaspoon cayenne pepper

2 dashes Tabasco™ sauce

¼ cup quartered artichoke hearts (about 2 to 3 canned artichoke hearts)

4 ounces fresh blue crabmeat

½ cup grated Parmesan cheese

Serves 8

Crab and Artichoke Dip

TWIGS BISTRO AND MARTINI BAR, KENNEWICK
CORPORATE CHEF JONATHAN HOLDEN

Hot crab dip is always popular for parties and on game days. This one, with Boursin® cheese and a kick from cayenne and Tabasco™, is especially good. Serve with grilled crostini, crackers, or crudité for dipping.

Preheat the oven to 375 degrees.

Heat a small skillet over medium heat and add the olive oil. Add the peppers and onions and cook until translucent, about 3 to 5 minutes, taking care not to brown the vegetables. Remove from the heat and let cool.

Combine the cream cheese, Boursin®, parsley, salt, pepper, garlic powder, cayenne, and Tabasco™ and mix until smooth. Add the peppers, onions, artichokes, and crabmeat and mix gently to combine.

Place the mixture into a baking dish and top with the Parmesan cheese. Bake, uncovered, until the mixture is golden brown and hot, about 20 minutes.

3 cups flour

1 teaspoon cayenne pepper
(or more if you prefer
more heat)

2 Walla Walla sweet onions

Salt

Peanut oil, for frying

Serves 4 to 8

Crispy Fried Walla Walla Sweet Onions

WHITEHOUSE-CRAWFORD RESTAURANT, WALLA WALLA
CHEF JAMIE GUERIN

Sweet onions from Walla Walla are well known throughout Washington and beyond, and nothing features them more prominently than these irresistible crispy fried onions. Although great as a snack, they're also a nice addition to top a steak or casserole.

Combine the flour and cayenne pepper in a large bowl. Slice the onions paper thin either on a mandoline or using a sharp knife. Dredge the onion slices in the flour and shake off excess flour using a strainer. Add peanut oil to a depth of 4 to 6 inches in a large stockpot and heat over medium–high heat.

Working in batches, place the onions in the oil and stir gently with metal tongs. When the onions are golden brown, use a strainer to remove the onions from the oil and place in a bowl lined with paper towels to drain. Season immediately with salt and repeat with the remaining onions. Serve hot.

¼ cup canola oil

½ teaspoon cumin seeds

1 cup chopped red onion
(about 1 medium onion)

1 tablespoon finely chopped
garlic (about 3 cloves)

½ cup finely chopped tomatoes
(about 1 medium tomato)

1 teaspoon salt

1 teaspoon crushed cayenne
pepper (optional)

½ teaspoon ground cumin
or garam masala

½ teaspoon ground fenugreek seeds
or mustard seeds (optional)
(see Sources on page 174)

Dash pepper

¼ cup plain yogurt (minimum
2% milk fat), stirred

8 eggs, hard cooked,
cooled to room temperature,
and peeled

1 teaspoon minced jalapeño
pepper, for garnish (optional)

Serves 8

Curried Deviled Eggs

SHANIK, SEATTLE ∞ CHEF MEERU DHALWALA

At Shanik, Chef Dhalwala serves Indian cuisine that is creative and daring, yet comforting, as you'll find in this Indian rendition of classic deviled eggs. Any remaining yolk filling can be covered and refrigerated for a few days, and tastes great as a sandwich spread or with crackers.

Heat the oil in a small pot on medium-high for 1 minute. Add the cumin seeds and allow them to sizzle until the seeds are dark brown but not black, about 30 seconds. Add the onion and sauté until golden, about 4 minutes. Add the garlic and sauté until golden brown, about 2 minutes. Stir in the tomatoes, and then add the salt, cayenne, cumin, fenugreek seeds, and pepper. Sauté for 4 to 5 minutes, and then remove from the heat.

To prevent curdling, place the yogurt in a small bowl and spoon some of the hot masala into the yogurt a tablespoon at a time, stirring well, until all of the yogurt and masala are combined.

Cut the eggs in half lengthwise and carefully scoop the yolks into a medium bowl. Mash the yolks with a fork, stir the warm masala mixture into the yolks, and mix well. Use a teaspoon or piping bag to stuff the egg white halves with the filling, and then sprinkle the minced jalapeño over the eggs. Serve immediately, or cover and refrigerate until chilled, about 30 minutes. Store extra eggs covered in the refrigerator for up to 3 days.

1 tablespoon extra virgin olive oil

¼ cup diced celery

¼ cup diced red onion

1 tablespoon diced red bell pepper

1 pound Dungeness crabmeat,
    picked of any shells or cartilage

1 tablespoon Dijon mustard

½ cup mayonnaise

1 cup saltine cracker crumbs

1 lemon, juiced

2 teaspoons Worcestershire sauce

2 tablespoons chopped parsley

½ teaspoon salt

¼ teaspoon pepper

Canola oil, for frying

Diced celery, red onion,
    and red pepper, for garnish
    (optional)

Serves 6

Dungeness Crab Cake

SIX SEVEN RESTAURANT, THE EDGEWATER HOTEL, SEATTLE
EXECUTIVE CHEF JOHN ROBERTS

Crab is the star ingredient in these cakes, with just enough other ingredients to add delicate flavor. Serve with an herbed cream sauce or tartar sauce.

Heat the oil in a medium skillet over medium heat. Add the celery, onion, and pepper, cook until soft, and then remove from the heat and cool.

Combine the cooked vegetables with the crabmeat, mustard, mayonnaise, cracker crumbs, lemon juice, Worcestershire, parsley, salt, and pepper and gently fold together. Refrigerate for 20 minutes to allow the cracker crumbs to absorb the liquid.

Heat a ½-inch layer of oil in a large skillet over medium heat. Shape the crab mixture into 6 round cakes and fry the crab cakes until cooked through, about 3 minutes per side. Garnish with diced vegetables and serve warm.

4 ounces shiitake mushrooms

1 live geoduck clam
    (see Sources on page 174)

¼ cup flour (see Note)

3 tablespoons butter, divided

4 cups baby spinach,
    loosely packed

1 tablespoon soy sauce

2 tablespoons sake

4 lemon wedges, for garnish

Serves 4

Geoduck Sauté

SUSHI KAPPO TAMURA, SEATTLE   ✍   CHEF TAICHI KITAMURA

Geoduck clams are favored around the world for their flavor and tender flesh and are imported from Washington to sashimi restaurants across Asia. If you happen across one in the local fish market, don't be intimidated by the large bi-valve, as they are actually quite easy to clean and prepare. If you can't find geoduck clams, you can substitute Manila, butter, or littleneck clams in this easy appetizer.

Remove the tough stems from the mushrooms; discard the stems and slice the caps. Clean the geoduck (*see Note*) and slice the flesh into thin, bite-sized pieces. Dredge the geoduck pieces in the flour and shake off extra flour.

Melt 1 tablespoon of the butter in a large sauté pan and sear the geoduck until golden brown, about 2 minutes, tossing the pieces as needed to cook evenly. Remove the geoduck and set aside.

Add the remaining butter to the pan and add the mushrooms. Cook until slightly softened, about 3 minutes, and then add the spinach, soy sauce, and sake and cook for another minute. Return the geoduck to the pan and toss together for 1 more minute. Serve warm with lemon wedges for squeezing over the top.

✍ **Note:** *Omit the flour for anyone with gluten sensitivities. To clean the geoduck, remove the rubber band holding the shell together and submerge the geoduck into a pot of boiling water for 15 seconds. Remove and immediately plunge the geoduck into an ice bath to cool it. Slide off and discard the loosened skin from the siphon, and then run a knife carefully around the open edges of the shell to remove the geoduck from the shell. Pull out and discard the stomach, and then cut the siphon on one side lengthwise to expose the inside. Rinse out any dirt or sand in the siphon and then proceed with the recipe.*

½ cup Grand Marnier

2 cups orange juice

1½ tablespoons dried
    orange zest powder

1 cup mayonnaise

Canola oil, for frying

20 prawns, peeled and
    deveined, tails on (16/20 size)

½ cup cornstarch

Serves 4

Grand Marnier Prawns

BARKING FROG, WILLOWS LODGE, WOODINVILLE
EXECUTIVE CHEF BOBBY MOORE

At the Barking Frog, one of the Northwest's most highly regarded restaurants, prawns are quick-fried before being tossed with this unusual Grand Marnier sauce. You can also simply boil or pan sear prawns and serve with the sauce for dipping.

Combine the Grand Marnier and orange juice in a saucepan over medium-high heat and simmer until the mixture is reduced to ½ cup, about 45 minutes; cool in the refrigerator. Combine the reduced, cooled Grand Marnier mixture with the orange zest powder and mayonnaise and refrigerate.

Add canola oil to a depth of ½ inch in a large sauté pan and heat over medium-high heat. Dust the prawns in the cornstarch, shaking off any excess. Working in small batches, fry the prawns until crispy, about 1 minute per side, and drain on paper towels. Toss the hot prawns with about half of the Grand Marnier mayonnaise to coat and serve hot. Serve additional sauce on the side for dipping.

Caper-parsley dipping sauce

⅔ cup extra virgin olive oil

6 tablespoons drained capers

6 tablespoons roughly chopped
    fresh parsley

6 anchovy fillets

¼ cup fresh lemon juice

2 large garlic cloves, halved

Salt and pepper

Halibut poppers

1 pound halibut fillets or scraps

2 tablespoons extra virgin olive oil

Salt and pepper

1 cup chopped green onions

3 tablespoons chopped fresh parsley

2 tablespoons flour

2 large garlic cloves, minced

1 lemon, zested

1 cup panko or fresh breadcrumbs,
    plus more for coating

2 eggs

½ cup milk

Canola or peanut oil, for frying

Halibut Poppers with Caper-Parsley Dipping Sauce

THE SHELBURNE INN, SEAVIEW   ∞   CHEF ROBERT ERICKSON

Poppers are a great way to use up pieces of halibut after you've trimmed a fillet into individual portions. The Shelburne Inn serves these savory nibbles on a bed of arugula with the dipping sauce on the side.

For the caper-parsley dipping sauce:
Combine the olive oil, capers, parsley, anchovies, lemon juice, and garlic in a food processor and blend until combined; season with salt and pepper to taste. The sauce can be made ahead and refrigerated until ready to use.

For the halibut poppers:
Preheat the oven to 400 degrees. Toss the halibut with the olive oil, spread in a single layer on a baking sheet, and season with salt and pepper. Bake the halibut until just firm to the touch, about 5 to 10 minutes.

Flake the cooked halibut and place it in a mixing bowl along with the green onions, parsley, flour, garlic, lemon zest, breadcrumbs, eggs, ½ teaspoon salt, and ¼ teaspoon pepper. Mix on low speed until just combined. Form mixture into 1-inch–diameter balls, dip in the milk, and then coat in additional breadcrumbs.

Add oil to a saucepan or deep frying pan to a depth of 1 inch and heat over medium–high heat to 350 degrees. The oil is at temperature when a bit of the halibut mixture sizzles in the oil. Place the poppers into the oil several at a time, taking care not to crowd the pan, and fry until just golden, about 1 to 2 minutes, turning to brown on all sides. Drain on a paper towel and repeat with the remaining poppers. Serve warm with the caper-parsley dipping sauce.

Serves 6 to 8

Celery seed aioli

2 egg yolks

2 tablespoons freshly squeezed
 lemon juice

2 garlic cloves, chopped

½ teaspoon kosher salt

Dash Tabasco™ sauce

¾ teaspoon celery seed

1 cup extra virgin olive oil

Celery salad

2 stalks celery, minced

1 tablespoon extra virgin olive oil

1 tablespoon lemon juice

1 tablespoon chopped fresh dill,
 or 1 teaspoon dried

½ teaspoon kosher salt

Pepper

Mussels

2 pounds fresh mussels, cleaned
 *(see Guidelines for Recipes
 on page xviii)*

½ cup dry white wine

½ cup flour

1 teaspoon sea salt

½ teaspoon pepper

Olive oil, for frying

Serves 4 to 6

Pan Fried Mussels
with Celery Salad

POPPY, SEATTLE   ✕   CHEF AND OWNER JERRY TRAUNFELD

*The "thali," a serving platter holding a variety of small dishes, is the
inspiration behind Chef Traunfeld's creative menu at Poppy. Serve the
mussels on the reserved half shells for a pretty presentation for a party
or buffet, or spread the salad on a platter, top with the mussels, and
serve with aioli to dip.*

For the celery seed aioli:
Put the egg yolks, lemon juice, garlic, salt, Tabasco™, and celery seed
in a blender. Turn the blender on and slowly pour in the olive oil in
a steady stream. Spoon into a small covered container and refrigerate
until ready to use.

For the celery salad:
Combine the celery, olive oil, lemon juice, dill, and salt in a small
bowl, mix together, and season with pepper to taste.

For the mussels:
Put the cleaned mussels in a large pot and pour the wine over them.
Turn the heat to high, cover, and cook the mussels until they are
all open, and then for an additional minute after that, about 3 to
4 minutes total. Drain the mussels in a colander, and then spread
them out on a baking sheet and refrigerate until cool.

Remove the meat from the shells, using a paring knife to aid if they
cling. Clean and wash the shell halves that don't have the mussel
attachment and reserve for serving the finished dish.

Mix the flour with the salt and pepper in a medium bowl. Dredge
the mussels in the seasoned flour and shake off the excess using a

(continued on page 46)

strainer. Pour a ¼-inch layer of olive oil into a large skillet over medium heat and add the mussels to the pan in a single layer. Cook until lightly browned on both sides, about 2 minutes. Drain the mussels on paper towels and sprinkle lightly with salt. Repeat with the remaining mussels.

To assemble:

Spoon about a teaspoon of the celery salad into each of the reserved shells and top with a fried mussel and a small dollop of aioli. The remaining aioli may be stored in the refrigerator for up to one week for use on sandwiches or in salads.

2 cups pomegranate juice

1 ½ cups minced shallots

¾ cup Champagne vinegar
or white wine vinegar

1 tablespoon freshly ground pepper

Yields 1 ½ cups

Pomegranate Mignonette Sauce for Freshly Shucked Oysters

TRACE, SEATTLE   CHEF STEVEN ARIEL

Fresh oysters are an absolute must when dining out in Washington, and Chef Ariel from Trace is partial to the Shigoku variety from Taylor Shellfish. The mignonette sauce may be prepared ahead of time and can be stored in the refrigerator for up to two weeks.

Pour the pomegranate juice into a medium saucepan over medium-high heat; bring to a simmer, reduce the heat, and cook until the juice has reduced to ½ cup. Combine the reduced juice with the shallots, vinegar, and pepper, mix well, and chill. To serve, spoon chilled mignonette sauce liberally over freshly shucked oysters.

Dough

2 cups flour

½ teaspoon salt

2 tablespoons cilantro puree
 (see Note)

½ cup warm water

Dumplings

¾ cup uncooked sweet brown rice

1 pound ground pork

3 tablespoons Vietnamese
 fish sauce

1 tablespoon chopped garlic

1 tablespoon chopped ginger

1 to 2 tablespoons kecap manis
 (see Note) (see Sources
 on page 174)

½ bunch cilantro, chopped

½ teaspoon ground mace

Chile sauce, for dipping

Peanuts, for garnish

Chopped cilantro, for garnish

Yields about 36 dumplings

Pork Cilantro Dumplings

REVEL, SEATTLE ❧ CHEF RACHEL YANG AND CHEF SEIF CHIRCHI

The dishes at Revel are inspired by Asian street food, like these classic pork dumplings that get a flavor boost from an infusion of cilantro in the dough. If you don't have the time to make your own dough, use pre-packaged wonton wrappers, which can be found in the produce section of most grocery stores. Extra dumplings may be frozen, uncooked, until needed.

For the dough:
Add the flour to a large bowl and stir in the salt. Combine the cilantro puree with the water and pour into the flour; mix together and knead until the dough becomes very smooth, about 3 minutes. Roll the dough until very thin, either on a floured board or through a pasta roller. Cut into 4-inch rounds using a cookie cutter.

For the dumplings:
Cook the rice according to the package directions and allow to cool. Combine the ground pork with the cooked rice, fish sauce, garlic, ginger, kecap manis, cilantro, and mace in a large bowl and mix all ingredients together. Place a heaping teaspoon of the filling onto each piece of dough, brush the edges with water, fold in half, and pinch closed to form the dumplings.

Place a steamer basket over an inch of simmering water. Spray the bottoms of the dumplings with cooking spray before placing them on the steamer basket. Working in batches, place dumplings into the steamer basket, cover, and steam for 5 minutes. If desired, pan sear the dumplings in canola oil after they are steamed to brown the bottoms. Serve hot dumplings with chile sauce for dipping, and garnish with peanuts and cilantro.

❧ *Note: To make cilantro puree, add a bunch of cilantro to a food processor and drizzle in canola oil or extra virgin olive oil with the blade running, just until the mixture forms a thick paste. Extra puree may be frozen. Kecap manis is a sweeter and thicker form of soy sauce. You can make it at home by combining ½ cup soy sauce with ⅓ cup palm sugar or dark brown sugar and simmering until reduced and thickened, about 15 minutes.*

5 egg yolks

1 ⅓ cups cream

½ cup grated Parmesan cheese

1 (8-ounce) wheel of Camembert cheese, rind removed, cubed

Pinch cayenne pepper

½ red jalapeño (or Fresno) chile, seeded and minced

Salt

Yields about 2 cups

Red Pepper Fonduta

TRACE, SEATTLE   CHEF STEVEN ARIEL

Located in the heart of Seattle, Trace was recently named one of the country's Best Hotel Restaurants by Food & Wine *magazine. This rich cheese spread is great on bread, toast, or crackers or served with your favorite crudité and pairs beautifully with wine. Chef Ariel uses Mt. Townsend Creamery or Kurtwood Farms cheeses when making fonduta in the restaurant.*

Whisk the yolks in a small bowl. Heat the cream in a small saucepan over medium-high heat until just scalding. Whisk a small amount of the hot cream into the eggs and when well incorporated, continue whisking in the remaining hot cream very slowly until completely mixed.

Pour the mixture back into the saucepan and add the Parmesan, Camembert, cayenne, and jalapeño. Cook over medium heat until the cheese is melted and the mixture is just thickened, about 5 minutes, and then cool over an ice bath. Cover and refrigerate until ready to serve. The fonduta may also be brought to room temperature before serving.

Scallop Crudo

BLIND PIG BISTRO, SEATTLE   ❧   CHEF CHARLES WALPOLE

This fresh and light appetizer boasts an explosion of interesting flavors. Chef Walpole prefers Alaskan weathervane scallops and uses a high-quality fleur de sel to finish the dish at the restaurant. Be sure to freeze the lime juice and zest in advance so that it's ready when serving the appetizer.

Place the lime zest and juice in a shallow container such as a pie pan and freeze.

Peel and dice the apple into ⅛-inch cubes and mix with the olive oil. Add the minced chile and chives to the apple. Mash the avocado until smooth and season with a bit of salt.

Slice each scallop horizontally into 4 thin slices. Place a spoonful of the apple mixture on each of four plates. Arrange 4 scallop slices (1 scallop) over the top of the apple and garnish with a dollop of avocado.

Sprinkle a bit of sea salt over the top, and then use a fork to grate the frozen lime mixture over the scallops; serve immediately.

3 limes, zested and juiced

1 green apple

2 tablespoons extra virgin olive oil

1 serrano chile, seeded and minced

1 tablespoon minced chives

1 ripe avocado

Sea salt

4 scallops (10/20 size)

Serves 4

12 oysters, freshly shucked
    or pre-shucked

½ cup semolina flour

Canola oil, for frying

2 teaspoons chopped fresh herbs
    (parsley, tarragon, chives,
    or fennel fronds)

Salt and pepper

Truffle mayonnaise, for dipping

Serves 1 to 2

Semolina Crusted Northwest Oysters

PRIMA BISTRO, LANGLEY, WHIDBEY ISLAND
CHEF AND OWNER SIEB JURRIAANS

At Prima Bistro they make fresh truffle mayonnaise to serve with these crunchy oysters. To make a quick version, combine ½ cup mayonnaise with 1 teaspoon Dijon mustard, 1 teaspoon lemon juice, 1 teaspoon white truffle oil, and a pinch of salt.

Toss the shucked oysters with the semolina until coated. Heat about ¼ inch of canola oil in a medium skillet over medium–high heat and fry the oysters until they just start to firm up and brown, about 2 to 3 minutes.

Toss the hot oysters with the herbs and season with salt and pepper. Serve hot oysters with truffle mayonnaise for dipping.

Salads & Sides

Strawberry Salad with Walnut Vinaigrette, p. 77

Vinaigrette

3 tablespoons minced garlic

3 tablespoons minced shallots

1 cup chopped rhubarb stalks
(or mashed fresh or frozen
strawberries)

¼ cup honey

¼ cup lavender flowers
(see Sources on page 174)

1 cup white balsamic vinegar

¼ cup thinly sliced mint

1½ cups extra virgin olive oil

Salt and pepper

Salad

1 (4-pound) seedless watermelon,
peeled and cut into
2-inch-thick slabs

Extra virgin olive oil

Salt and pepper

12 cups arugula or baby spinach

6 ounces crumbled feta cheese

Mint leaves, for garnish

Bacon-Wrapped Scallops on Watermelon and Feta Salad with Lavender-Rhubarb Vinaigrette

GORDON'S ON BLUEBERRY HILL, FREELAND, WHIDBEY ISLAND
EXECUTIVE CHEF GORDON STEWART

The unusual combination of lavender and rhubarb creates a dazzling dressing for watermelon. If rhubarb is not in season, you may substitute fresh or frozen strawberries. Be sure to presoak the bamboo skewers in water before you grill the scallops so they don't burn on the grill.

For the vinaigrette:
Combine the garlic, shallots, rhubarb, honey, and lavender in a medium saucepan over medium heat and cook until the rhubarb breaks down. Let cool.

Combine the rhubarb mixture with the vinegar and mint and puree in a blender; strain and discard the solids. Slowly whisk the olive oil into the rhubarb mixture, and then season with salt and pepper to taste.

For the salad:
Heat the grill to high heat. Brush the watermelon slices with olive oil and season with salt and pepper. Grill on both sides for just a few seconds to mark the outside but not to cook the center. Remove from the grill and refrigerate.

For the scallops:
Preheat the oven to 375 degrees and heat the grill to high heat.

Lay the bacon slices on two rimmed baking sheets and cook in the oven until partially cooked, about 10 to 12 minutes, taking care to remove the bacon before it gets completely crisp. Drain on paper towels until cool enough to handle.

Scallops

24 thick slices of quality
　　applewood-smoked bacon

24 large scallops (U/10 size)

6 (10-inch) wooden skewers,
　　soaked in water

Extra virgin olive oil

Serves 6

Wrap each scallop around the edge with a strip of partially cooked bacon and place 4 bacon-wrapped scallops on each skewer. Brush the scallops lightly with olive oil and grill until the scallops are cooked through and the bacon is crispy, about 3 minutes per side, making sure to have a squirt bottle handy to keep flames down on the grill.

To assemble:
Cut the cooled watermelon into large cubes and coat with the desired amount of the dressing. Lay the arugula on a platter and lay the watermelon cubes on top of the arugula. Top with the feta cheese and garnish with fresh mint leaves, and then place the skewers of scallops over the top. Serve immediately.

1 pound seedless grapes
  (about 3 cups)

1 large shallot, thinly sliced

1 tablespoon extra virgin olive oil

1 tablespoon balsamic vinegar

1 tablespoon minced
  fresh rosemary

Salt and pepper

Serves 4 to 6

Balsamic and Rosemary Roasted Grapes

COOKING WITH MICHELE　❧　MICHELE MORRIS

Grapes are one of the top ten commodities grown in Washington State and are in season from late summer through November. These simple roasted grapes can be served on their own as an interesting side dish, used on top of crostini with Boursin® or Brie cheese for a sweet and savory appetizer, or mixed into wild rice for a stunning side dish.

Preheat the oven to 375 degrees. Toss the grapes in a medium bowl with the shallot, olive oil, vinegar, and rosemary and then spread on a rimmed baking sheet. Sprinkle lightly with salt and pepper. Roast the grapes until heated through and slightly shriveled, about 15 to 20 minutes. Serve warm or at room temperature.

3 cups water

½ cup Lapsang souchong
    black tea leaves
    (see Sources on page 174)

1 cup Beluga lentils
    (see Sources on page 174)

1 (3-inch) piece of kombu
    (see Sources on page 174)

2 teaspoons canola oil

½ onion, diced

1 tablespoon whole cumin seed

2 teaspoons salt

Serves 2

Black Tea Infused Beluga Lentil Dhal

SUTRA, SEATTLE   ❧   CHEF COLIN PATTERSON

Chef Patterson uses Lapsang souchong smoked black tea leaves in this classic lentil dish, but you may substitute another type of black tea. Kombu helps to remove the gaseous quality from legumes, although it doesn't add much flavor and can be left out if desired. This dhal has a pronounced cumin flavor, so if you're not a fan of cumin, reduce the amount used.

Bring the water to a boil in a medium stockpot, and then remove from the heat, add the tea, and allow the tea to steep for about 10 minutes. Strain and discard the tea leaves.

Add the lentils and kombu to the tea broth, cover, and simmer until the lentils are soft, but not mushy, about 15 minutes.

While the lentils are cooking, heat the oil in a medium skillet over medium-high heat and add the onion. Sauté until the onion is soft and lightly browned, about 3 to 5 minutes; add the cumin and sauté for another minute.

When the lentils are cooked, remove the kombu and discard it; stir in the salt. Combine the onion and ½ cup of the lentils in a blender and puree together, adding a bit of the cooking liquid or water as needed to obtain a smooth puree. Add the puree back into the lentils, stir together, and serve.

Vinaigrette

¼ cup balsamic vinegar,
    preferably an aged variety

⅓ cup extra virgin olive oil

2 tablespoons agave syrup

½ tablespoon sea salt

½ teaspoon pepper

1 tablespoon chopped fresh basil

¼ teaspoon chopped garlic
    (about 1 small clove)

Salad

4 cups water, divided

1 cup uncooked farro

1 cup uncooked quinoa,
    rinsed several times

½ cup thinly sliced figs

½ medium apple

3 tablespoons chopped
    fresh fennel bulb
    (about ½ of a small bulb)

3 tablespoons chopped fresh mint

3 tablespoons chopped fresh basil

¼ cup dried cranberries

¼ cup candied pecans,
    broken into medium pieces
    (see Note)

Serves 8

Farro and Fig Salad

PLUM BISTRO, SEATTLE ❧ CHEF MAKINI HOWELL

*Makini Howell has made a name for herself at her popular vegan res-
taurant in Seattle, Plum, but this robust salad is sure to be loved by meat
eaters as well. Chef Howell uses fresh figs at the restaurant, but you may
rehydrate dried figs if you can't get fresh ones. Adjust the portions of apple,
fennel, herbs, and cranberries to suit your own taste.*

For the vinaigrette:
Combine the vinegar, olive oil, agave syrup, salt, pepper, basil,
and garlic in a container with a tight-fitting lid. Cover and shake
well to blend.

For the salad:
Bring 2 cups of water to a boil in a medium saucepan and add
the farro. Cover, reduce the heat to simmer, and cook until all of
the water is absorbed and the farro has blossomed, about 20 to
30 minutes. While the farro is cooking, bring the remaining 2 cups
of water to a boil in another saucepan and add the quinoa.
Cover, reduce the heat to simmer, and cook until the quinoa is
fluffy, about 15 minutes. Remove both from the heat, combine
the cooked grains in a large bowl, and cool.

When the grains have cooled, add the figs to the grains. Roughly
chop the apple and add it to the grains, along with the fennel, mint,
basil, cranberries, and pecans. Toss with the dressing and serve
either at room temperature or refrigerate.

❧ *Note: To make candied pecans, melt ¼ cup sugar in a small saucepan
over medium heat until it takes on a light golden color. Remove from the
heat, stir in the pecans, and then pour the mixture onto a baking sheet lined
with a silicone liner or parchment paper. Allow the nuts to cool completely,
and then break into medium-sized pieces.*

Flans

4 tablespoons butter, plus more
    for buttering the dishes

1 small onion, peeled and
    thinly sliced (about 1 cup)

2 cups shelled fresh or frozen
    green peas

½ cup heavy cream

4 eggs

1 teaspoon salt

Sautéed pea vines and morel mushrooms

½ cup chicken broth

2 tablespoons Chinese oyster sauce

1 teaspoon cornstarch

2 tablespoons extra virgin olive oil

½ pound small fresh
    morel mushrooms

Kosher salt and pepper

½ pound tender young pea vines
    or spring greens, rinsed

Serves 6

Green Pea Flans with Sautéed Pea Vines and Morel Mushrooms

RESTAURANT MARCHÉ, BAINBRIDGE ISLAND
CHEF AND OWNER GREG ATKINSON

Chef Atkinson learned to make vegetable flans under the French master Roger Vergé. Although peas are wonderful when in season, he has found that carrots, winter squash, or cauliflower can produce excellent results in other seasons.

For the flans:
Preheat the oven to 400 degrees. Butter six 6-ounce soufflé dishes and place them into a large baking dish or two smaller baking dishes.

Heat a large skillet over medium heat, add the butter to melt, and cook the onion, stirring often, until tender, about 5 minutes. Add the peas and cream, bring the mixture to a boil, cover, and reduce the heat to low. Simmer gently just until the peas are heated through, about 3 to 5 minutes.

Add the eggs and salt to a blender or food processor and pulse, and then add the cooked pea mixture. Cover the top of the machine with a kitchen towel to protect your hand from the heat, and then pulse until the mixture is smooth.

Fill the ramekins evenly with the pea mixture and pour boiling water into the baking dish around the ramekins until it reaches halfway up the sides. Cover each ramekin with a buttered circle of parchment paper, and then cover the entire baking dish with aluminum foil. Bake until a knife inserted in the center of a ramekin comes out clean, about 25 to 30 minutes.

(continued on page 60)

For the sautéed pea vines and morel mushrooms:
Stir the chicken broth, oyster sauce, and cornstarch together and set aside. Heat a large sauté pan over medium–high heat. Add the olive oil and the morels, sauté until the mushrooms are heated through, about 2 minutes, and season with salt and pepper to taste.

Add the pea vines and use a pair of tongs to move the greens quickly around the pan just long enough to distribute the oil evenly over the surface of the vegetables, about 1 minute. Add the chicken broth mixture all at once to the hot pan. Toss quickly until the liquid is reduced to a shiny glaze, about 1 minute.

To assemble:
Run a knife or spatula around the edges of the flans to loosen them from the dishes and then invert onto plates. Spoon the sautéed pea vines and morel mushrooms onto the plates with the flans and serve immediately, or hold in a 180–degree oven for up to an hour before serving.

Dressing

2 ounces anchovies (1 small tin)

1 tablespoon Dijon mustard

1 egg

1 egg yolk

1½ cups canola oil

2 garlic cloves, roughly chopped

2 hard cooked eggs,
    roughly chopped

1 tablespoon capers, chopped

¼ cup chopped parsley

2 tablespoons red wine vinegar

1 lemon, zested and juiced

Salt and pepper

Salad

2 large heads of romaine,
    quartered lengthwise into
    8 pieces (see Note)

Extra virgin olive oil

½ cup toasted pine nuts

2 ounces anchovy fillets (1 small tin)

½ cup shaved hard cheese
    (such as Parmesan, Tuada,
    or Pecorino)

16 large croutons

Serves 8

Grilled Romaine Salad

MATT'S IN THE MARKET, SEATTLE   ❧   EXECUTIVE CHEF SHANE RYAN

Grilling lettuce is easy and creates an interesting texture for salads. Chef Ryan's dressing is similar to a classic Caesar dressing, but he enhances it with chopped eggs, capers, and parsley.

For the dressing:
Combine the anchovy fillets, mustard, egg, egg yolk, canola oil, and garlic in the bowl of a food processor and whirl until completely smooth and thick. Spoon into a bowl and stir in the hard cooked eggs, capers, parsley, vinegar, lemon zest, and lemon juice, and season with salt and pepper to taste.

For the salad:
Brush the romaine quarters with olive oil and grill for 1 to 2 minutes per side. Lay grilled romaine on a large serving platter (or plate individually) and drizzle with the desired amount of dressing. Top with pine nuts, anchovy fillets, cheese, and croutons.

❧ **Note:** *Many stores sell hearts of romaine, which are smaller than full heads of romaine lettuce. If you use hearts of romaine in this recipe, you'll need 4 heads, each cut in half lengthwise, for 8 servings.*

2 large russet potatoes,
    peeled and shredded

2 teaspoons kosher salt

2 teaspoons freshly squeezed
    lemon or lime juice

Pepper

3 green onions, chopped

1 large shallot, chopped

2 tablespoons chopped fresh
    flat-leaf parsley

½ teaspoon Old Bay® Seasoning

¼ cup grated Parmesan cheese

½ cup breadcrumbs

2 eggs, beaten

4 tablespoons unsalted butter

¼ cup extra virgin olive oil

Yields 8 latkes

Latkes

BENNETT'S, MERCER ISLAND
CHEF AND OWNER KURT DAMMEIER

For eggs benedict at Bennett's, they replace the English muffin with these latkes, but latkes are equally good on their own as a side dish for breakfast, lunch, or dinner.

Combine the potatoes, salt, and juice in a medium bowl and let stand for 5 minutes. Place the potatoes into a clean dishtowel and squeeze to remove as much excess liquid as possible.

Dry the bowl and return the potatoes to the bowl. Add the pepper, green onions, shallot, parsley, Old Bay®, cheese, breadcrumbs, and eggs and use your hands to mix everything together.

Heat a large skillet over medium heat and add half of the butter and half of the olive oil. Shape ½-cup portions of the potato mixture into 4-inch patties. Cook 4 of the patties in the skillet at one time until they are golden brown on the first side, about 4 minutes. Using a thin spatula, turn the patties over and cook until golden brown on the second side, about 3 to 5 more minutes. Remove to a serving plate. Add the remaining butter and olive oil to the skillet and cook the remaining patties. Serve warm.

❧ *Note: If you need to reheat latkes to serve, place them on a baking sheet in a 350-degree oven until heated through and crisp.*

4 slices prosciutto

1 tablespoon sea salt, divided

2 bay leaves

1 whole live lobster
   (about 2 pounds) *(see Note)*

2 blood oranges

2 shallots, sliced in thin rings

1 Japanese or English cucumber

3 tablespoons rice vinegar

½ teaspoon cracked
   coriander seeds

1 teaspoon pepper

2 tablespoons sugar

2 heads Belgian endive

1 tablespoon finely
   chopped tarragon

2 tablespoons crème fraîche
   or sour cream

1 tablespoon extra virgin olive oil

Serves 4

Lobster, Endive, and Orange Salad

CRUSH, SEATTLE ❧ CHEF JASON WILSON

This is a perfect salad for special occasions, with interesting flavor combinations and impressive ingredients like lobster and prosciutto. Chef Wilson prefers blood oranges in the dish, but you may substitute any variety of orange if you can't find blood oranges.

Preheat the oven to 450 degrees. Spray a sheet pan with cooking spray and lay the strips of prosciutto on the pan. Bake the prosciutto until crisp, about 10 minutes, taking care not to burn. Cool at room temperature to create prosciutto chips.

Fill a medium stockpot two-thirds full with water, add 1 teaspoon of salt and the bay leaves, and bring to a boil. Using tongs, plunge the live lobster into the pot, cover, and remove from the heat. Allow the lobster to cook in the hot water for 12 minutes. Remove the lobster from the water and when cool enough to handle, remove the meat from the claws and body, cut the meat into large chunks, and refrigerate until ready to serve.

Segment the oranges, reserving the juice. Pour the blood orange juice over the shallots and marinate for 10 minutes. Thinly slice the cucumber and toss with the vinegar, coriander, pepper, and sugar. Slice the endive into large chunks, break apart into individual pieces, and place in a large bowl.

Drain the juices from the shallots and cucumbers into a small bowl. Add the remaining salt, tarragon, crème fraîche, and olive oil to the drained juices and whisk together to make the dressing. Combine the shallots and cucumbers with the endive and toss with the dressing.

To assemble:
Plate the salad on a large platter or divide among four plates. Top with the cooked lobster, orange segments, and prosciutto chips.

❧ **Note:** *If you don't have access to a live lobster or don't have the inclination to cook one, you may use ½ pound precooked lobster meat instead.*

¼ cup blanched Marcona
   almonds *(see Sources
   on page 174)*

1 pound Lopez Island grown
   arugula or other high-quality
   arugula

4 teaspoons lemon juice

¼ cup extra virgin olive oil

½ teaspoon salt

½ teaspoon pepper

¼ cup grated Parmesan cheese,
   divided

Serves 8

Lopez Arugula Salad

THE BAY CAFÉ, LOPEZ ISLAND   ❧   CHEF AND OWNER TIM SHEA

Featuring locally grown arugula, this salad at The Bay Café is brilliant in its simplicity. Pair it with any roast meat for a dinner salad, or top with chicken or fish for a lunch entrée. The dressing is very light, so if you prefer more dressing, just add additional lemon juice and olive oil.

Preheat the oven to 450 degrees. Toast the almonds on a baking sheet until lightly browned, about 10 minutes, and then cool and chop.

Toss the arugula in large bowl with the lemon juice, olive oil, salt, pepper, and half of the Parmesan cheese. Divide the arugula among eight plates and garnish with the remaining Parmesan cheese and chopped almonds. Serve immediately; the salad will wilt rapidly once it is dressed.

Lemon vinaigrette

½ cup freshly squeezed
  lemon juice

½ cup extra virgin olive oil

2 teaspoons sugar

1 teaspoon salt

Pinch red chili flakes

Farro salad

⅓ cup uncooked farro

½ to 1 cup shredded Napa cabbage

½ to 1 cup shredded romaine lettuce

1 tablespoon finely chopped
  fresh Italian parsley

1 tablespoon finely chopped
  fresh mint

1 rounded tablespoon chickpeas

1 tablespoon toasted pumpkin
  seeds *(see Note)*

1 tablespoon dried currants

2 tablespoons crumbled feta cheese

Yields 1 entrée salad or 2 side salads

Mediterranean Farro Salad

BACKDOOR KITCHEN, FRIDAY HARBOR, SAN JUAN ISLAND
CHEFS AND OWNERS LEE AND SASHA HILDERMAN

The Backdoor Kitchen, in an unassuming location on San Juan Island, has been described as the kind of local's secret spot that travelers dream of discovering. The Hildermans use organic ingredients in this hearty salad wherever possible.

For the lemon vinaigrette:
Combine the lemon juice, olive oil, sugar, salt, and chili flakes in a small covered container and shake well to combine. Shake again just before using to ensure the vinaigrette is mixed well.

For the farro salad:
Fill a medium saucepan half full with salted water and bring to a boil. Add the farro, cover, reduce the heat to simmer, and cook until tender but not mushy, about 20 minutes. Drain the farro and place it in a bowl to cool.

Combine the cooled farro with the cabbage, lettuce, parsley, mint, chickpeas, pumpkin seeds, currants, and feta cheese and toss with desired amount of the lemon vinaigrette.

❧ **Note:** *The restaurant tosses pumpkin seeds in Bragg Liquid Aminos (see Sources on page 174) and bakes them in a 400-degree oven until they smoke and turn dark brown. You may follow this technique or simply roast them until browned.*

Mushroom Fondue in Sweet Dumpling Squash

GORDON'S ON BLUEBERRY HILL, FREELAND, WHIDBEY ISLAND
EXECUTIVE CHEF GORDON STEWART

Serving the fondue in colorful squash bowls is a playful way to present this dish. If you prefer, skip the squash entirely and serve the warm mushroom fondue in a fondue pot for a group.

2 sweet dumpling or carnival squash, cut in half

½ cup chopped shallots

¼ cup minced garlic

2 cups vegetable stock

2 cups heavy cream

3 tablespoons extra virgin olive oil

1 pound chanterelle mushrooms, roughly chopped

4 tablespoons butter

2 tablespoons chopped fresh herbs (chives, thyme, or rosemary), divided

¼ cup flour

1½ cups dry sherry

2 cups grated Gruyère cheese

Toast points

Serves 4

Remove the seeds from the squash and carefully carve out the meat in the center, taking care not to leave a hole in the bottom; reserve the squash meat. Heat a large soup pot of water to boiling and blanch the squash bowls for 2 minutes in the hot water. Remove the squash from the water and refrigerate.

Roughly chop the squash meat that was scooped out of the shells and add it to a medium soup pot. Add the shallots, garlic, stock, and cream and place the pot over medium-high heat. Bring to a low boil and cook until the liquid has reduced by half. Strain the mixture and discard the solids. Reserve the reduced cream mixture.

Heat a large sauté pan over medium-high heat and add the olive oil. Add the mushrooms and cook until the mushrooms release their moisture and cook down, about 10 to 15 minutes. When the moisture from the mushrooms has evaporated, add the butter and herbs, reserving just a bit of herbs to garnish the fondue. When the butter has melted, stir in the flour until incorporated and cook for 2 minutes, taking care not to burn the flour. Remove from the heat, add the sherry, and whisk until creamy and the flour is well incorporated.

Return the pan to the heat and slowly whisk in the reserved cream mixture. When the sauce is heated thoroughly and has thickened, add the Gruyère cheese and stir until melted. Ladle the fondue into the squash bowls, garnish with herbs, and serve with toast points.

5 to 6 cups low-sodium chicken stock

1 tablespoon extra virgin olive oil

2 tablespoons butter

1 small onion, finely chopped

2 garlic cloves, minced

1 pound mushrooms, sliced
(a variety, like button,
portobello, and oyster,
works well)

2 cups Arborio rice

½ teaspoon ground coriander

½ cup dry white wine

¼ cup heavy cream

½ cup grated Parmesan cheese

½ cup chopped fresh parsley,
divided

Kosher salt and pepper

Serves 6

Mushroom Risotto

CHRISTOPHER'S ON WHIDBEY, COUPEVILLE, WHIDBEY ISLAND
CHEF AND PARTNER ANDREAS WURZRAINER

After many years preparing four-star meals in elegant restaurants across the world, Chef Wurzrainer relocated his family to Whidbey Island in 2002 and purchased Christopher's, a favorite with locals and visitors alike. Chef Wurzrainer serves this classic risotto dish with his Pepper and Goat Cheese-Filled Chicken Breast (see recipe on page 127).

Pour the stock into a medium stockpot and bring to a simmer; keep hot while you prepare the risotto.

Combine the oil and butter in a large, heavy-bottomed saucepan and heat over medium-high heat. Add the onions and garlic and sauté for 2 minutes. Add the sliced mushrooms and sauté, stirring occasionally, until their liquid is evaporated and they begin to brown, about 15 minutes.

Add the rice and coriander and stir for 1 minute before adding the white wine, stirring to pick up any browned bits from the bottom of the pan. Let the rice cook until the wine is nearly evaporated. Add 1 cup of the chicken stock and stir constantly until the liquid is nearly evaporated. Continue adding ½ cup of stock at a time, stirring until nearly evaporated, just until the rice is tender and the risotto is creamy, about 20 to 30 minutes. You may not need to use all of the stock.

Stir in the cream, Parmesan cheese, and half of the chopped parsley. Mix well and season with salt and pepper to taste. To serve, pour the risotto onto a large serving platter and top with the remaining chopped parsley.

Potatoes

3 pounds small fingerling potatoes, halved if large

¼ cup extra virgin olive oil

6 whole serrano chiles

1 teaspoon salt

¼ teaspoon pepper

1 bunch green onions, thinly sliced, for garnish (optional)

Spicy tomato sauce

¼ cup extra virgin olive oil

1 Spanish onion, diced

4 garlic cloves, thinly sliced

1 to 2 serrano chiles, diced (remove seeds if you prefer less heat)

3 tablespoons brown sugar

2 (28-ounce) cans crushed tomatoes

Salt

Red wine vinegar

Aioli

2 egg yolks

4 garlic cloves, minced

1 cup extra virgin olive oil

2 teaspoons lemon juice

Salt and pepper

Patatas Bravas with Spicy Tomato Sauce and Garlic Aioli

SAFFRON MEDITERRANEAN KITCHEN, WALLA WALLA
CHEF CHRIS AINSWORTH

This dish can be found in some variation in almost every tapas bar in Barcelona, which inspired the chef to add it to the menu at Saffron, where it has since become a classic. Freeze any extra tomato sauce for another use.

For the potatoes:
Adjust the oven rack to the lowest position and heat the oven to 450 degrees.

Toss the potatoes with the oil, chiles, salt, and pepper. Place the potatoes cut side down and chiles on a rimmed baking sheet and roast until tender and golden brown, about 20 to 30 minutes.

For the spicy tomato sauce:
Heat a medium saucepan over medium heat and add the olive oil. Add the onion and garlic and cook until soft and lightly browned, about 5 minutes. Add the chiles and brown sugar and cook 5 minutes more. Add the tomatoes and bring to a boil. Reduce the heat and simmer for 30 minutes, stirring often. Coarsely puree the sauce with a stick blender or in a food processor, and season with salt and vinegar to taste. The sauce may be stored for up to 1 week in the refrigerator or up to 6 months in the freezer.

For the aioli:
In a medium bowl, beat the egg yolks with a wire whisk until light and fluffy and then stir in the garlic. Gradually whisk in the oil in a thin stream, whisking constantly until light and creamy. Stir in the lemon juice, season with salt and pepper to taste, and refrigerate until ready to use.

Brava salt

2 tablespoons kosher salt

1 teaspoon whole cumin seed

1 teaspoon whole coriander seed

3 tablespoons spicy Spanish paprika
   (or regular paprika)
   (see Sources on page 174)

3 tablespoons sweet Spanish
   paprika (or regular paprika)
   (see Sources on page 174)

½ teaspoon cayenne pepper

Serves 8

For the brava salt:
Combine the salt, cumin seed, and coriander seed in a spice grinder and process until fine. Combine the mixture with the two types of paprika and the cayenne pepper. Store in a covered container in the pantry.

To assemble:
Spread spicy tomato sauce on the bottom of a large serving platter. Sprinkle the roasted potatoes generously with the brava salt and then place the potatoes on top of the spicy tomato sauce in the serving platter. Garnish with the roasted chiles and green onions and serve with the aioli sauce for dipping.

1 cup red grapes, halved

1 cup white grapes, halved

3 tablespoons honey

1 tablespoon Champagne vinegar

¼ cup extra virgin olive oil

1 cup diced feta cheese

3 tablespoons chopped chives

Salt and pepper

4 cups arugula or baby
   lettuce leaves

Serves 4

Red and White Grape Salad with Feta Cheese

LUC, SEATTLE & CHEF THIERRY RAUTUREAU/CHEF IN THE HAT™

A simple combination of fruit and cheese is transformed into a robustly flavored dish when tossed with a sweet vinaigrette. Serve the marinated grapes and feta cheese from this recipe without any greens for an interesting appetizer or on top of greens for a salad course.

Toss the grapes with the honey, vinegar, and olive oil and marinate in the refrigerator for 2 hours. Combine the marinated grapes with the feta cheese and chives and season with salt and pepper to taste.

To serve, divide the arugula among four plates and top with the marinated grapes and feta cheese. If desired, serve family style on one large platter.

1 ½ pounds whole beets
(any color), cleaned
and tops removed

3 tablespoons red wine vinegar,
divided

Salt

⅓ cup extra virgin olive oil

½ teaspoon Dijon mustard

½ teaspoon salt

¼ teaspoon pepper

4 cups baby arugula

Serves 4

Roasted Beet Salad

THE SHELBURNE INN, SEAVIEW
CHEF ROBERT ERICKSON

At the inn, this salad is served with roasted halibut. The entire dish is drizzled with a white wine and orange marmalade sauce and then topped with thinly sliced basil.

Preheat the oven to 350 degrees.

Place the beets in a baking dish and add ¼ inch of water. Cover tightly with aluminum foil and bake until the beets are easily pierced with a skewer, about 45 minutes.

When the beets are cooked, remove the foil and allow them to cool. When cool, place the baking dish in the sink under running water and rub the skins off; discard the skins.

Cut the peeled beets into wedges and place in a bowl, keeping the red beets separate if you are using multicolored beets. Toss the beets with 1 tablespoon of the red wine vinegar (divide between the red beets and others if using multicolored beets) and a dash of salt, and allow the beets to rest for 30 minutes. Beets can be prepared to this point and stored in the refrigerator for up to 1 day until ready to use.

While the beets are resting, combine the olive oil, 2 tablespoons red wine vinegar, mustard, salt, and pepper in a small covered container and shake well to combine. Toss the beets with the dressing and serve over a bed of arugula.

1½ pounds trimmed Northwest albacore tuna loin

Salt and pepper

6 tablespoons extra virgin olive oil, divided

1 tablespoon kosher salt

1 pound fresh green beans, trimmed

1 pound Yukon Gold potatoes (about 2 medium potatoes)

2 tablespoons red wine vinegar

1 head Bibb lettuce, torn, rinsed, and spun dry

4 hard cooked eggs, peeled and quartered lengthwise

1 cup pitted Niçoise or Saracena olives

1 pint cherry tomatoes, halved

Extra virgin olive oil, for garnish

Red wine vinegar, for garnish

Sea salt and pepper

Serves 4

Salade Niçoise

RESTAURANT MARCHÉ, BAINBRIDGE ISLAND
CHEF AND OWNER GREG ATKINSON

Technically speaking, a Niçoise is a woman from Nice, but in culinary terms, the moniker is inextricably linked to this substantial salad made with tuna and produce typically found in farmers' markets in the south of France. This Pacific Northwest version features a wild albacore tuna loin that's seared rare, not canned.

Cut the tuna loin into 4 equal pieces and season with salt and pepper. Heat 2 tablespoons of the olive oil in a large skillet over medium-high heat. Sear the fish on all sides, turning as soon as the fish is cooked about a quarter of an inch inward, about 30 seconds on each side. The tuna should be browned on the surface and cold inside. Remove the tuna and allow it to rest.

Heat a large stockpot of water over high heat until boiling and add the kosher salt. Add the green beans and cook until they are bright green and slightly tender, about 4 minutes. Lift the beans out of the water with a slotted spoon and spread them on a baking sheet in a single layer to cool. Reserve the pot of boiling water to cook the potatoes.

Peel the potatoes, cut them into 1-inch dice, and add them to the boiling water. Cook until the potatoes are tender but not falling apart, about 10 minutes. Lift the potatoes out of the boiling water with a slotted spoon and transfer them to a large mixing bowl. Whisk the remaining 4 tablespoons of olive oil with the red wine vinegar and toss the warm potatoes with the mixture (they will absorb some of the dressing).

Distribute the lettuce evenly among four plates and top each with a piece of tuna. Arrange small mounds of the dressed potatoes, bundles of green beans, the hard cooked eggs, a few pitted olives, and the cherry tomatoes around the tuna and drizzle additional olive oil and vinegar over the salads as desired, making sure to get some on the tuna as well. Sprinkle sea salt and pepper all around and serve.

Kimchi paste

¼ cup fish sauce

¼ cup roughly chopped fresh ginger

15 garlic cloves

⅓ cup Korean red pepper powder
(see Note) (see Sources
on page 174)

2 teaspoons Korean salted shrimp
(optional) (see Sources
on page 174)

3 tablespoons sugar

Brussels sprouts

3 tablespoons sesame oil

2 pounds Brussels sprouts,
stems removed and cut in half

¼ to ½ cup water

Serves 4 to 6

Sautéed Brussels Sprouts with Kimchi Flavors

LLOYDMARTIN, SEATTLE   ✎   CHEF AND OWNER SAM CRANNELL

Asian flavors are featured prominently in restaurants around the Pacific Northwest, such as the kimchi seasonings used in this recipe at Chef Crannell's highly regarded Queen Anne restaurant.

For the kimchi paste:

Combine the fish sauce, ginger, and garlic in a blender and mix well. Combine the puree with the pepper powder, salted shrimp, and sugar and mix until a paste forms. Store the kimchi paste in the refrigerator for up to a month.

For the Brussels sprouts:

Heat a large sauté pan over high heat and add the sesame oil. Add the Brussels sprouts and sauté until they start browning, about 3 minutes. Reduce the heat to low and add 2 to 4 tablespoons of the kimchi paste and the water. Stir to make sure the sprouts are coated and continue cooking until the sprouts are tender, about 3 more minutes. Serve with any roast meat or fish.

✎ **Note:** *A mixture of 2 parts medium hot chili powder and 1 part smoked paprika can be substituted for the Korean pepper powder.*

2 tablespoons Champagne
    vinegar or white wine vinegar

½ cup walnut oil

Salt and pepper

12 cups loosely packed mixed
    salad greens

2 cups strawberries,
    hulled and quartered

¼ cup sliced almonds, toasted

2 ounces crumbled goat cheese
    (or more if desired)

Serves 6

Strawberry Salad
with Walnut Vinaigrette

CAFÉ FLORA, SEATTLE ✦ OWNER NAT STRATTON-CLARKE

Café Flora uses baby salad greens, trimmed watercress, arugula, goat cheese, and strawberries from local producers Tieton Farm & Creamery and Hayton Farms. Keep this salad bookmarked for those occasions when you need to quickly pull together a pretty salad for company.

Whisk together the vinegar and oil in a small bowl and season with salt and pepper to taste.

Put the salad greens in a large mixing bowl and toss with desired amount of dressing, reserving at least 2 tablespoons of the dressing for the berries. Divide the salad greens among six chilled salad plates.

Put the strawberries in the bowl used to toss the greens and toss with the reserved vinaigrette. Adjust the salt and pepper if needed and toss again.

Tuck the dressed strawberries among the leaves on each plate to distribute them evenly. Scatter each salad with almonds, top with goat cheese, and serve immediately.

4 tablespoons butter, divided

¼ cup chopped shallots

10 cups chopped Swiss chard,
    including stems (about 1 large
    or 2 medium bunches)

1½ teaspoons kosher salt

2 tablespoons flour

1 cup milk

2 tablespoons coarsely chopped
    fresh oregano

½ cup dried currants or
    dried cranberries

Salt and pepper

¼ cup plus 2 tablespoons
    breadcrumbs, divided

¼ cup freshly grated
    Parmesan cheese

1 tablespoon melted butter

Serves 4

Swiss Chard Gratin with Oregano and Currants

POPPY, SEATTLE   &   CHEF AND OWNER JERRY TRAUNFELD

Although Chef Traunfeld may have a reputation for creating dishes with globally inspired flavors, this easy gratin is more an example of simple comfort food that happens to be special enough to share with company.

Preheat the oven to 375 degrees.

Melt 2 tablespoons of the butter in a large saucepan over medium heat. Add the shallots and stir for a minute, then add as much chard as will comfortably fit in the pan; add the kosher salt. Toss the chard with tongs until it wilts down, and then keep adding more chard until it is all wilted. Transfer the chard to a strainer set over a bowl and press down on it with a rubber spatula to press out excess moisture.

In the same saucepan, melt 2 tablespoons of butter and whisk in the flour to form a roux. When the roux bubbles, pour in the milk all at once and whisk until the sauce boils and thickens, about 1 to 2 minutes. Stir in the wilted chard, oregano, and currants and season with salt and pepper to taste.

Spray four 6-ounce custard dishes with cooking spray and sprinkle ½ tablespoon of the breadcrumbs in the bottom of each, shaking to distribute the breadcrumbs evenly. Spoon the chard mixture into the custard dishes. Mix the remaining ¼ cup of breadcrumbs with the Parmesan cheese and the melted butter and sprinkle it over the tops of the custard dishes. Bake until bubbly and browned, about 25 minutes, and serve hot.

1 ½ pounds apples, peeled,
cored, and cubed
(about 4 to 6 apples)

½ cup water

1 teaspoon ground cinnamon

Serves 4 to 6

Warm Cinnamon Applesauce

COOKING WITH MICHELE ❧ MICHELE MORRIS

Washington grows nearly every variety of apple imaginable; some are best eaten fresh and raw, while others are favored for cooking. Braeburn, Cortland, Gravenstein, and McIntosh are among the Northwest's favorites for pies and applesauce. Warm applesauce is great with Roast Rack of Pork (see recipe on page 141) or simply as a snack or light dessert.

Combine the apples with the water and cinnamon in a medium saucepan. Bring to a boil, cover, reduce to simmer, and cook until the apples are soft, about 20 minutes. Mash or puree to desired consistency and serve. Leftovers may be refrigerated and may be rewarmed or served cold.

Balsamic vinaigrette

½ cup balsamic vinegar

1 teaspoon Dijon mustard

1 medium garlic clove, minced

1 small shallot, minced

1 teaspoon kosher salt

¼ teaspoon pepper

1 cup extra virgin olive oil

Salad

8 ounces baby spinach
    (about 4 cups)

2 ounces sliced crimini mushrooms

3 tablespoons brown sugar

½ cup cooked and crumbled bacon

½ cup diced tomato

3 hard cooked eggs, chopped

½ cup toasted pecan pieces
    (optional)

Serves 4

Wilted Spinach Salad

KEENAN'S AT THE PIER, THE CHRYSALIS INN AND SPA, BELLINGHAM
EXECUTIVE CHEF ROB HOLMES

With a wonderful combination of wilted spinach and mushrooms, this is the salad to make when you want something warming. The hard cooked eggs and bacon are the perfect complement to the wilted greens, while the pecans add a nice crunch.

For the balsamic vinaigrette:
Combine the balsamic vinegar, mustard, garlic, shallot, salt, pepper, and olive oil in a covered container and shake well to emulsify.

For the salad:
Place the spinach in a salad bowl and set aside. Combine 1 cup of the vinaigrette with the sliced mushrooms, brown sugar, and bacon bits in a heavy-bottomed pan over medium-high heat and cook until the sugar melts, the dressing starts to bubble, and the mushrooms begin to wilt, about 3 minutes.

Remove from the heat and add the mushroom mixture to the spinach, tossing to combine. The dressing will slightly wilt the spinach as you toss it. Divide evenly among four plates and top with the tomato, chopped eggs, and toasted pecans. Store extra vinaigrette in the refrigerator for up to a week.

"World's Best" Mac & Cheese

BENNETT'S, MERCER ISLAND
CHEF AND OWNER KURT DAMMEIER

Chef Kurt Dammeier, who also owns Beecher's Handmade Cheese in Seattle, says that every day he wakes up thinking about what to cook for dinner. He uses his Flagship and Just Jack cheeses in his popular mac & cheese dish at Bennett's.

8 ounces penne pasta

4 tablespoons unsalted butter

5 tablespoons flour

1 ½ cups milk

8 ounces grated Beecher's Flagship cheese or sharp white cheddar cheese (about 2 cups) *(see Sources on page 174)*

2 ounces grated Beecher's Just Jack cheese or Monterey Jack cheese (about ½ cup) *(see Sources on page 174)*

½ teaspoon kosher salt

¼ teaspoon chili powder

⅛ teaspoon garlic powder

Serves 4

Preheat the oven to 350 degrees. Butter a 2-quart baking dish or spray it with cooking spray.

Heat a large pot of salted water to boiling and cook the penne 2 minutes less than the package directions specify. (It will finish cooking in the oven.) Rinse the pasta in cold water and set aside.

Melt the butter in a heavy-bottomed saucepan over medium heat and whisk in the flour. Continue whisking and cooking for 2 minutes. Slowly add the milk, whisking constantly, and then cook, stirring frequently, until the sauce thickens, about 8 minutes.

Remove from the heat and add 1¾ cups of Flagship cheese, ¼ cup of Just Jack cheese, salt, chili powder, and garlic powder. Stir until the cheese is melted and all the ingredients are incorporated, about 3 minutes.

Combine the cooked pasta and the cheese sauce in a medium bowl and mix thoroughly. Pour into the prepared baking dish and sprinkle the top with the remaining cheese.

Bake, uncovered, for 20 minutes, and then remove from the oven and let stand for 5 minutes before serving.

2 tablespoons butter

½ tablespoon extra virgin olive oil

½ yellow onion, finely diced

1 tablespoon salt

1 tablespoon finely chopped
  rosemary

2 cups heavy cream

2¼ cups chicken stock

2 cups uncooked polenta

2 tablespoons grated Romano
  cheese

1 teaspoon pepper

2 tablespoons chopped
  fresh parsley

Canola oil, for frying

Serves 8

Yellow Corn Grit Cakes

CAFE NOLA, BAINBRIDGE ISLAND
CHEF AND OWNER KEVIN WARREN

Chef Warren serves pan-seared scallops with a red pepper sauce over these corn cakes, but you can top them with virtually any fish, shellfish, vegetable, or sauce you like, or even serve them as a side dish instead of rice or potatoes.

Heat the butter and oil in a large stockpot over medium-high heat until sizzling. Add the onions and salt, reduce the heat to medium, and cook the onions until soft, about 5 minutes. Add the rosemary, cream, and stock and bring to a boil. Slowly add the polenta in a steady stream while whisking.

Continue whisking until the polenta begins to thicken, and then stir the polenta with a rubber spatula until fully cooked, about 10 to 15 minutes depending on the coarseness of the grain. Stir in the cheese, pepper, and parsley, and adjust the salt if needed.

Spray a 13 x 9 x 2-inch baking dish with cooking spray and spoon the polenta into the baking dish. Spread the polenta evenly with a spatula and cool in the refrigerator. When cooled, cut the polenta into 8 pieces.

Heat a large skillet over medium-high heat and add 2 to 3 table-spoons of canola oil. Fry polenta pieces two at a time until lightly browned on both sides, about 5 minutes. Remove to a baking sheet lined with paper towels and repeat until all the polenta is fried. Serve warm.

Soups & Stews

Lyon Style Onion Soup, p. 94

½ cup (1 stick) butter

¾ cup flour

4 cups water

1 ounce crab base *(see Note)*
    (see Sources on page 174)

8 ounces heavy cream

2 tablespoons Johnnie Walker
    Red Label

⅛ teaspoon cayenne pepper

1 teaspoon salt

1 teaspoon pepper

1 tablespoon tomato paste

8 ounces crabmeat,
    picked of any shells

¼ cup chopped chives

Serves 4

AQUA Spicy Crab Bisque

AQUA BY EL GAUCHO, SEATTLE
CORPORATE EXECUTIVE CHEF AND OWNER KEN SHARP,
AQUA BY EL GAUCHO EXECUTIVE CHEF STEVE CAIN

It's hard to resist a rich, filling crab soup like this one. Serve it with a simple salad and some crusty bread for an easy lunch or dinner.

Heat a large stockpot over low heat, add the butter, and whisk in the flour until incorporated to form a roux. Cook over low heat for 10 to 15 minutes, stirring occasionally, and taking care not to burn the roux.

Combine the water, crab base, cream, Johnnie Walker, cayenne, salt, pepper, and tomato paste and whisk into the roux. Simmer until thickened, stirring often.

Warm four soup bowls in the oven. Add 2 ounces of crabmeat to each bowl and ladle the hot soup over the crabmeat. Alternatively, stir the crabmeat into the soup before serving. Garnish with chopped chives.

❧ ***Note:*** *To easily make your own crab base, crack the legs, claws, and top shell of a whole, cooked Dungeness crab and place the pieces in a medium stockpot; cover with 4 cups of water. Dice a small onion, 1 carrot, and 1 stalk of celery and add them to the pot along with ½ cup white wine, 1 bay leaf, a few peppercorns, and 1 tablespoon of tomato paste. Simmer, uncovered, for 1 to 2 hours, and then strain and discard the solids. Continue to simmer until the liquid is reduced to 1 cup. Use the full cup in place of the crab base in this recipe.*

1 to 2 pounds asparagus spears
(see Note)

1 tablespoon extra virgin olive oil

1 tablespoon butter

2 medium shallots, roughly chopped

3 to 4 cups chicken stock
(see Note)

8 ounces Brie cheese

1 cup heavy cream

Salt and pepper

Fresh thyme, for garnish

Serves 6

Asparagus and Brie Soup

COOKING WITH MICHELE   ❧   MICHELE MORRIS

Farmers in Washington's Columbia Basin produce about 22 million pounds of asparagus each year. This simple yet elegant soup starts with an asparagus base, then adds creamy Brie cheese for a punch of rich flavor.

Remove the tough ends from the asparagus spears and cut into 1-inch pieces. Heat a medium stockpot over medium-high heat and add the olive oil and butter. When the butter has melted, add the asparagus and shallots and sauté for 3 minutes. Add the stock, bring to a boil, cover, reduce heat, and simmer for 15 minutes.

Remove and discard the rind from the Brie. Break the Brie into chunks and add to the soup. Once the Brie has melted, puree the soup using an immersion blender or working in batches in a traditional blender. Return the soup to the stove, add the cream, and simmer for 5 minutes. Season with salt and pepper to taste, garnish with fresh thyme, and serve warm.

❧ **Note:** *Larger spears of asparagus have larger tough ends. You'll have more asparagus for the soup after removing the tough ends if you use thinner spears. Use more stock if you prefer a thinner, creamy soup resembling the texture of bisque; use less stock if you prefer a thicker soup with a more pronounced asparagus flavor.*

3 medium beets, any color

4 heirloom tomatoes
(about 2 pounds),
peeled and seeded

2 cucumbers, peeled and seeded

1 sweet onion

2 medium sweet peppers

1 small handful fresh basil

1 small handful fresh mint

¾ cup extra virgin olive oil

¼ cup red wine vinegar

Salt and pepper

Extra virgin olive oil, for garnish

Serves 8

Beet Gazpacho

WHITEHOUSE-CRAWFORD RESTAURANT, WALLA WALLA
CHEF JAMIE GUERIN

Chef Guerin advises that this dish is best prepared when the markets are full of the very freshest garden produce. Be sure to use only sweet vine-ripened tomatoes for the best flavor in this soup.

Preheat the oven to 400 degrees. Roast the beets until fork tender, about an hour, and then remove and cool.

When cool enough to handle, peel the beets and cut them into 1-inch cubes. Roughly chop the tomatoes, cucumbers, onion, and peppers and place them in a large bowl. Add the beets, basil, mint, olive oil, and vinegar and stir to coat. Let stand at room temperature for an hour for the flavors to meld.

Working in batches, puree the mixture in a blender until smooth. Season the soup with salt and pepper to taste and chill well. Garnish with a drizzle of extra virgin olive oil to serve.

12 Totten Virginica oysters

4 tablespoons butter, divided

1 small onion, minced

1 small head cauliflower,
    broken into small florets

2 cups Prosecco

½ cup heavy cream

Salt and pepper

1 bunch sorrel or 1 cup
    baby spinach, chopped

Serves 4

Cauliflower and Prosecco Soup with Warm Totten Virginica Oysters and Sorrel

HOW TO COOK A WOLF, SEATTLE   ❧   CHEF ETHAN STOWELL

Chef Stowell has turned a simple cauliflower soup into something special with the addition of Prosecco, fresh oysters, and sorrel. The soup is strained before serving at the restaurant for a silky texture, but you may omit this step at home.

Shuck the oysters, reserving the liquid, and hold the oysters in the refrigerator until ready to use.

Heat a medium stockpot over medium heat. Add 2 tablespoons of the butter and the onions and cook until the onions are soft and translucent, about 3 to 4 minutes. Add the cauliflower, Prosecco, reserved oyster liquid, and heavy cream and bring to a boil. Reduce to a simmer, cover, and cook until the cauliflower is tender but not mushy, about 8 to 10 minutes.

Puree the soup in a blender or using a stick blender and season with salt and pepper to taste. Return the soup to the pot and keep warm.

Heat the remaining butter in a small pan over medium heat and add the shucked oysters; heat until warmed through, about 2 to 4 minutes. Divide the soup among four warm soup bowls, place three warm oysters in each bowl, and sprinkle the sorrel over the top. Serve immediately.

1 pound dried corona beans

2 garlic cloves

3 tablespoons extra virgin olive oil

4 medium carrots, sliced

2 medium yellow onions, diced

5 stalks celery, sliced

2 bay leaves

2 dried cherry peppers (optional)

1 head garlic, cloves separated
    and thinly sliced

½ bottle dry white wine

1 Parmesan rind (optional)

1 bunch curly kale, cleaned
    and torn apart

1 quart stock (chicken, beef, or veal)

3 lemons, juiced

Sea salt and pepper

Olive oil, for finishing

Serves 8

Corona Bean Soup

LA MEDUSA, SEATTLE
CHEFS AND OWNERS GORDON WISHARD AND MEREDITH MOLLI

This hearty vegetable soup is big on flavor and nutrition thanks to an array of aromatics, an entire bunch of kale, and beans. If you can't find corona beans, you may substitute large lima beans (shell them after soaking them), gigante beans (common in Italy), or cannellini beans. Using stock enriches the flavor, but you may make the soup vegetarian by using vegetable broth instead.

Place the beans in a large stockpot and cover with water 4 inches over the top of the beans. Soak the beans overnight.

The following day, drain the beans, place them back in the pot, and cover with water. Add 2 whole garlic cloves, cover, and cook slowly over low heat until the beans are tender, about 2 hours. Store the beans in the refrigerator in their liquid until ready to use. The beans may be cooked a day or two in advance.

Heat a large stockpot over medium heat and add the olive oil. Add the carrots, onions, celery, bay leaves, and cherry peppers. Cook, stirring often, until the vegetables begin to soften, about 5 to 10 minutes.

Add the sliced garlic and cook just until fragrant, about 1 minute more. Add the wine and cook until the liquid is reduced by at least half, about 5 minutes.

Drain the beans, discard the garlic cloves, and add the beans to the stockpot along with the Parmesan rind, kale, and stock. Bring to a simmer and cook gently for 20 minutes. Add the lemon juice and season with salt and pepper to taste. Remove bay leaves and drizzle with olive oil just before serving.

½ pound red-skinned potatoes

1 dozen freshly shucked medium
    oysters, juice reserved
    (or 1 small jar of extra-small
    oysters)

¾ cup (1½ sticks) unsalted butter

½ link chorizo sausage,
    casing removed and
    meat crumbled

3 medium leeks, chopped

1 teaspoon sea salt

1 tablespoon Old Bay® Seasoning

¾ cup flour

3 quarts half-and-half

12 ounces Dungeness crabmeat,
    picked clean

1 ear corn, kernels cut from the cob

½ cup seeded and diced tomato,
    for garnish

¼ cup chopped parsley,
    for garnish

Serves 16

Crab and Oyster Chowder

PIKE PLACE CHOWDER, SEATTLE
CHEF AND OWNER LARRY MELLUM

Each day, Pike Place Chowder creates eight, house-made, fresh chowders, taking inspiration from the fish markets and produce stands in Pike Place Market, which provide a wealth of possibilities for creating new and interesting chowders. Many of their chowders are already award winning, like this one that helped them win first place in the 2012 West Coast Chowder Cook-Off, and others are destined to become so.

Boil or microwave the potatoes until tender, and then chill them under cold running water and dice into ½-inch pieces. Chop the oysters into bite-sized pieces, retaining the juice.

Heat a large stockpot or Dutch oven over medium-high heat and add the butter. When the butter has melted, add the chorizo and leeks and sauté until the leeks are translucent, about 5 minutes. Stir in the salt and Old Bay® Seasoning.

Sprinkle flour over the mixture and stir until incorporated. Slowly whisk in the half-and-half until all of the flour and half-and-half are well combined. Continue stirring until the soup is heated to just barely simmering. Add the diced potatoes, oysters, reserved oyster juice, crabmeat, and corn kernels and continue to heat until thickened, taking care not to bring the chowder to a full boil and stirring continuously to prevent scorching.

For best results, let the chowder cool in the refrigerator for one day, allowing the ingredients to meld. Reheat to warm, not hot, before serving. To serve, ladle into bowls and garnish with diced tomato and chopped parsley.

4 thyme sprigs

4 tablespoons butter

1 tablespoon canola oil

8 ounces shiitake mushrooms, sliced

¾ cup diced yellow onions

½ cup diced celery

½ cup diced carrots

¼ cup flour

⅓ cup sherry

1 cup stock or water

2 cups heavy cream or half-and-half

1 teaspoon freshly squeezed
lemon juice

1 teaspoon kosher salt

Serves 6

Cream of Mushroom Soup

LAKE QUINAULT LODGE, QUINAULT   CHEF BRADLEY HARRIS

This grand lodge along Lake Quinault was built in 1926 and remains an enchanted retreat from the busy pace of the modern world. Their decadent mushroom soup, which cooks up in about 20 minutes, can be made with half-and-half if you'd like to reduce the fat.

Remove the thyme leaves from the stems and discard the stems. Heat a large stockpot over medium–high heat and add the butter and canola oil. When the butter melts, add the mushrooms, onions, celery, carrots, and thyme leaves and sauté for 5 minutes, stirring occasionally. Add the flour and stir until the flour is completely absorbed into the other ingredients, about a minute.

Add the sherry and stock, and use a whisk to stir constantly for 1 to 2 minutes to fully cook out the raw flour taste. Add the heavy cream, bring to a simmer, reduce the heat, and cook for 5 minutes while stirring constantly.

Stir in the lemon juice, add the salt, and then puree to the desired consistency using a stick blender or a traditional blender. Serve hot with a simple green salad for a light meal.

2 tablespoons extra virgin olive oil

1 red onion, diced

4 garlic cloves, minced

½ pound mild Italian pork sausage

2 large carrots, peeled
and chopped

2 cups Joseph's Grainery Lentils,
rinsed *(see Sources on
page 174)*

5 (14.5-ounce) cans beef broth

1 (28-ounce) can diced tomatoes
with juice

2 tablespoons tomato paste

2 teaspoons chopped
fresh rosemary

1 teaspoon dried oregano

1 cup packed fresh spinach

Salt and pepper

Grated Parmesan cheese,
for garnish

Serves 8

Lentil and Sausage Soup

JOSEPH'S GRAINERY, COLFAX

*The rolling Palouse hills, in southeastern Washington, claim to be the pea
and lentil capital of the world. After seventy years (and five generations)
in business, Joseph's Grainery began selling products directly to consumers
via the Internet, so now everyone can enjoy their bounty.*

Heat a large stockpot over medium–high heat and add the olive oil.
Add the onion and sauté until translucent, about 3 to 5 minutes. Add
the garlic and the sausage and cook, stirring occasionally, until the
sausage is browned. Add the carrots and cook for 3 more minutes,
and then add the lentils.

Cook the lentils for a few minutes, and then add the beef broth,
tomatoes, tomato paste, rosemary, and oregano. Bring to a boil, cover,
reduce the heat to low, and simmer for 30 minutes.

Add the spinach and simmer for 10 more minutes, adding more
broth or water if the soup becomes too thick, and season with salt
and pepper to taste. Serve soup with grated Parmesan cheese and
some nice crusty bread.

Lyon Style Onion Soup

LE PICHET, SEATTLE
EXECUTIVE CHEF AND CO-OWNER JIM DROHMAN

"Gratin Lyonnais," typical in the city of Lyon in Burgundy, differs from the French onion soup found in restaurants in Paris in that it is made with chicken stock instead of beef stock. It yields a soup that is lighter and features the flavor of the onions, while still remaining very satisfying. Chef Drohman recommends serving the soup with a robust village-designated Beaujolais, such as a Morgon or Moulin a Vent.

4 tablespoons unsalted butter

2½ pounds yellow onions, thinly sliced

4 cloves garlic, thinly sliced

1½ cups sherry

¾ cup dry white wine

1 teaspoon finely chopped thyme leaves

1 bay leaf

6 cups chicken stock

Salt and pepper

6 large croutons *(see Note)*

2 cups grated Gruyère cheese (about ½ pound)

Serves 6

Heat a large soup pot over medium heat and add the butter. When the butter melts, add the onions and garlic and cook, stirring often, until the onions are a rich brown color, about 45 minutes.

Add the sherry, increase the heat, and cook until it is almost completely reduced. Add the white wine and reduce by half. Add the thyme, bay leaf, and chicken stock and simmer for 20 minutes; season with salt and pepper to taste.

Remove the bay leaf, spoon the soup into six individual bowls, and top each with a crouton. Spread the cheese over the croutons and heat under the broiler until crusty and golden, about 2 to 3 minutes. Serve immediately.

❧ ***Note:*** *To make the croutons, bake ½-inch-thick slices of hearty bread on a sheet pan in a 350-degree oven until dry and crisp, about 5 minutes.*

Croutons *(see Note)*

8 (1-inch-square) brioche pieces

Extra virgin olive oil

Soup

6 cups water

½ cup sugar

1 tablespoon salt

2 pounds shucked English peas
   (see Note)

1 tablespoon extra virgin olive oil

1 medium onion, diced small

1 tablespoon fresh tarragon leaves

8 mint leaves

¼ cup parsley leaves
   (large stems removed)

2 cups chicken stock

2 ounces salmon roe, for garnish
   (optional)

Pea shoots or pea leaves,
   for garnish (optional)

1 lemon, zested, for garnish
   (optional)

Extra virgin olive oil, for garnish

Serves 4

Pea Soup with Brioche Croutons

MATT'S IN THE MARKET, SEATTLE ❧ EXECUTIVE CHEF SHANE RYAN

The garnish of croutons, roe, lemon, and pea shoots turns this otherwise simple pea soup into a work of art.

For the croutons:
Preheat the oven to 400 degrees. Toss the brioche croutons with olive oil; spread them on a baking sheet and bake until golden brown, about 7 to 10 minutes, and then set aside to cool.

For the soup:
Combine the water, sugar, and salt in a large stockpot over high heat and bring to a boil. Add the peas and blanch for 3 minutes, and then drain the peas and chill them in an ice bath.

Heat the olive oil in a sauté pan over medium heat and cook the onion until translucent, about 5 minutes. Working in batches if necessary, combine the onion, peas, tarragon, mint, parsley, and chicken stock in a blender or food processor and puree. If the mixture is too thick, add some water until the mixture is smooth.

To assemble:
Pour the pea soup into four bowls; garnish each with 2 brioche croutons, the salmon roe, pea shoots, lemon zest, and olive oil. Soup may be served warm or chilled.

❧ **Note:** *You may use store-bought croutons in place of the homemade brioche croutons if desired. Although this soup is wonderful made with fresh spring peas, you may also make it with high-quality frozen peas.*

2 cups sliced peaches

¼ cup peeled, seeded,
and sliced English cucumber

¼ cup diced red pepper

2 tablespoons diced dried apricots

1 garlic clove, slightly crushed

2 tablespoons honey

¼ cup extra virgin olive oil

¼ cup white balsamic vinegar

Salt and pepper

Crème fraîche, for garnish

Diced cucumber, for garnish
(optional)

Serves 2 to 4

Peach Gazpacho

CANLIS, SEATTLE   ❧   EXECUTIVE CHEF JASON FRANEY

At Canlis, a restaurant with a long list of awards and accolades (it's often called the top restaurant in Seattle), this rich gazpacho is served as a small tasting portion before the meal. It will feed two as a lunch portion of soup.

Combine the peaches, cucumber, red pepper, apricots, garlic, and honey in a large bowl. Toss the mixture with the olive oil and vinegar and season with salt. Place in a covered plastic or glass container and refrigerate overnight.

Remove the garlic clove from the mixture and discard it, and then puree the soup in a blender. Chill the soup and season with salt and pepper to taste. To serve, ladle the soup into bowls and garnish with crème fraîche and diced cucumber.

Roasted Butternut Squash Bisque with Dungeness Crab

LUNA, SPOKANE   EXECUTIVE CHEF ZACH STONE

This rich and creamy soup is perfect for a cool fall day. Leftovers (without the crab garnish) freeze well.

4 pounds butternut squash

Extra virgin olive oil

Salt and pepper

¾ pound carrots, chopped

¾ pound yellow onions, chopped

2 cups heavy cream

¼ cup light brown sugar

½ tablespoon kosher salt

1 tablespoon chopped fresh ginger

¼ teaspoon cayenne pepper

1 teaspoon ground mace

1 pound Dungeness crabmeat, picked clean, for garnish (optional)

Serves 12 to 16

Preheat the oven to 375 degrees. Cut the squash in half lengthwise, scoop out the seeds, and discard the seeds. Rub the cut side of the squash with olive oil and season with salt and pepper. Lay the squash cut side down on a baking sheet lined with foil and roast until soft, about 45 minutes. Remove from the oven and let cool slightly.

While the squash is cooling, heat a large stockpot over medium heat and add 2 tablespoons of olive oil. Add the carrots and onions and cook slowly until the vegetables are tender, about 15 minutes.

Scoop out the flesh from the cooled squash and add it to the vegetables. Add hot water just to cover the vegetables, cover, bring to a simmer, and cook for 30 minutes. Add the cream, brown sugar, salt, ginger, cayenne, and mace and simmer the soup for 10 more minutes. Puree using a stick blender or in a traditional blender until very smooth, and season with salt and pepper to taste. To serve, ladle the soup into large bowls and top with crabmeat.

½ pound red-skinned potatoes (about 8 small potatoes)

¾ cup (1 ½ sticks) unsalted butter, divided

1 medium yellow onion, chopped

4 celery stalks, chopped

1 teaspoon coarsely ground black pepper

2 tablespoons garlic powder

¾ cup flour

6 cups water

6 cups half-and-half

1 (8-ounce) package cream cheese, softened and cut into 1-inch chunks

¾ cup capers, well rinsed

1 (6-ounce) can tomato paste

1 ½ pounds smoked salmon (lox or cold smoked), broken into chunks

Salt

Serves 8 to 10

Smoked Salmon Chowder

PIKE PLACE CHOWDER, SEATTLE
CHEF AND OWNER LARRY MELLUM

The rich, briny flavors of this Pacific Northwest favorite bring rave reviews from locals as well as visitors from all over the world. The chowder is best prepared a day ahead and reheated to warm before serving with warm bread and a medium-bodied white wine.

Boil or microwave the potatoes until just tender and then cool them under running water. Dice potatoes into ½-inch chunks and set aside.

Heat a large stockpot over medium-high heat and melt 2 tablespoons of the butter; add the onions and celery and sauté until translucent, about 5 minutes. Stir in the pepper and garlic powder. Add the remaining butter, let it melt, then lower the heat and gradually add the flour until it is incorporated into the butter. Add the water and simmer for 3 minutes.

Stir in the half-and-half, cream cheese, capers, and tomato paste. Heat the chowder mixture to near-boiling over medium heat and then add the salmon and potatoes. Stir gently until the mixture thickens but do not boil the soup; season with salt to taste.

Main
Courses

Ossobuco with Salt-Roasted Fingerling Potatoes p. 119

5 ounces applewood-smoked bacon
or regular bacon,
cut into ¼-inch pieces

½ pound ramps or small leeks

½ cup (1 stick) unsalted butter,
divided

4 ounces morel mushrooms,
cleaned and halved
(or quartered, if large)

1 small shallot, minced

1 small garlic clove, minced

1 teaspoon minced fresh thyme

1¾ cups fish stock

1 pound skinless halibut fillet,
cut into 4 portions

Salt and freshly ground
white pepper

Extra virgin olive oil, for garnish

Serves 4

Baked Halibut with Morels, Ramps, and Smoked Bacon Butter Sauce

LUC, SEATTLE ❧ CHEF THIERRY RAUTUREAU/CHEF IN THE HAT™

The use of fish stock combined with smoked bacon butter sauce produces a tender and savory piece of fish that pairs perfectly with the morel mushrooms.

Heat a medium skillet over medium-high heat and cook the bacon until crispy and browned, 5 to 7 minutes, stirring occasionally. Drain the fat and set the bacon aside.

Trim the root ends from the ramps and cut each ramp in half where the white gives way to the green tops. Cut the white portions into ¼-inch pieces and leave the ramp greens whole. If using leeks, trim to the white and pale green portion, then halve crosswise, cut into ¼-inch wide strips, and rinse well to remove any sand.

Preheat the oven to 350 degrees.

Heat a medium skillet over medium-high heat and melt 2 table-spoons of the butter until slightly nutty smelling, taking care not to burn the butter. Add the morels and sauté for 30 seconds. Add the white portion of the ramps (or all of the leeks), shallot, garlic, and half of the thyme and sauté, stirring often, until the ramps begin to soften, about 2 to 3 minutes.

Add three-quarters of the bacon, the ramp greens, and 1¼ cups of the fish stock to the skillet. Bring just to a boil, and then simmer until reduced by three-quarters, about 8 to 10 minutes. Add 4 tablespoons of the remaining butter, swirling the pan so it melts into the sauce; keep warm over very low heat.

Pour the remaining ½ cup of fish stock in a large oven-safe skillet and warm over medium heat. Whisk in the remaining 2 tablespoons of butter and add the remaining bacon and remaining thyme. Season the halibut pieces with salt and pepper and add them to the skillet. Spoon some of the cooking liquid over the fish, and then place the entire pan in the oven. Bake just until nearly opaque through the center, about 10 minutes, basting with the cooking liquid once or twice.

When the fish is cooked, remove it to a warm platter, pour the halibut cooking liquids into the pan with the sauce, and bring to a low boil. Season the sauce with salt and pepper to taste.

To serve, spoon some of the ramps, bacon, mushrooms, and sauce onto warmed plates. Top with the halibut pieces and spoon the remaining sauce over the fish. Drizzle olive oil around and serve immediately.

Black Bean Quinoa Burger

BONNEVILLE HOT SPRINGS RESORT AND SPA, NORTH BONNEVILLE
EXECUTIVE CHEF EDWARD J. TIPPEL III

Chef Tippel recommends serving these hearty vegetarian burgers on a brioche bun with smoked pepper jack cheese.

¼ cup uncooked quinoa,
    rinsed several times

½ cup water

2 tablespoons extra virgin olive oil,
    divided

1 tablespoon butter

10 ounces crimini mushroom
    caps, quartered

½ white onion, diced

1 garlic clove, minced

½ cup corn kernels

¼ pound Yukon gold potatoes,
    peeled, cooked, and mashed

3 cups black beans *(see Note)*

1 tablespoon ground cumin

1 teaspoon finely chopped
    fresh oregano

¼ cup chopped cilantro

Salt and pepper

2 eggs *(see Note)*

½ cup breadcrumbs *(see Note)*

¼ cup extra virgin olive oil

Serves 6

Combine the quinoa and water in a small saucepan over high heat and bring to a simmer. Cover, reduce the heat, and simmer until fluffy and the water has all been absorbed.

While the quinoa is cooking, heat 1 tablespoon of the olive oil and the butter in a large sauté pan over medium-high heat. Add the mushrooms and cook, stirring occasionally, until the mushrooms are nicely browned, about 15 minutes.

While the mushrooms cook, heat the remaining tablespoon of olive oil in a medium skillet over medium heat. Add the onion and sauté until lightly browned. Add the garlic and corn and cook for 1 more minute.

Combine the quinoa, mushrooms, onions, garlic, corn, mashed potatoes, and black beans in a large bowl. Add the cumin, oregano, and cilantro, use a fork to mix well, and then season with salt and pepper to taste. Add the eggs and breadcrumbs and stir to combine. Divide the mixture into six portions and press into patties; refrigerate for at least 2 hours to help the patties hold their shape while cooking.

Heat 2 tablespoons of olive oil in a large skillet over medium heat. Add 3 of the patties and cook until golden brown, about 4 minutes per side, turning carefully with a thin metal spatula so that the patties don't crumble. Remove to a warm platter, add the remaining olive oil, and cook the remaining patties. Serve on buns with desired toppings.

❧ **Note:** *If you use dried black beans like Chef Tippel, begin with 1 cup dried black beans and soak them in a large pot of water overnight. The next day, drain and rinse the beans, return them to the pot, add water to cover 4 inches over the beans, and simmer until tender, 1 to 2 hours. Chef Tippel does not include eggs or breadcrumbs in his burgers, but adding them helps hold the burgers together while cooking.*

½ pound fingerling potatoes

1 bay leaf

2 sprigs fresh thyme

1 teaspoon sea salt

4 (6-ounce) black cod fillets, deboned, preferably with the skin on

Salt and pepper

Extra virgin olive oil

3 leeks, sliced and rinsed clean

4 garlic cloves, minced

6 anchovy fillets, minced

1 cup water

1 cup dry white wine

1 pound Manila clams
   (see Note on page 104)
   (see Sources on page 174)

¼ teaspoon chili flakes

1 tablespoon minced fresh Italian parsley

1 lemon, for garnish

Serves 4

Black Cod with Fingerling Potatoes and Manila Clams

LA MEDUSA, SEATTLE
CHEFS AND OWNERS GORDON WISHARD AND MEREDITH MOLLI

La Medusa serves "Sicilian-inspired food for the soul." This recipe requires three pans: one large enough to hold the fish, another with a lid to cook the clams, and a third to sauté the potatoes.

Place the potatoes, bay leaf, thyme, and sea salt in a medium stockpot and cover with water. Heat over high heat until the water begins to boil, and then reduce the heat to simmer and cook until the potatoes can be easily pierced with the tip of a knife, about 10 minutes. Drain, discard the bay leaf and thyme, and cool the potatoes. Once the potatoes are cool, slice into ¼-inch coins. Potatoes may be prepared the day before.

Preheat the oven to 450 degrees. Season the fish with salt and pepper. Heat a large oven-safe skillet over medium-high heat. Add a small coating of olive oil to the pan and place the fish skin side down in the pan. Weight the fish down using a small plate to ensure a browned crust. Cook for 2 minutes, remove the plate weight, and then transfer the entire skillet to the bottom rack of the oven. Do not turn the fish. Cook until the fish fillets are cooked through, but not dried out, about 10 minutes.

While the fish is cooking, heat another skillet over medium-high heat and add 2 tablespoons of olive oil along with the potato coins and sliced leeks. Season with salt and pepper and sauté until heated through and lightly browned, about 5 minutes.

(continued on page 104)

While the potatoes and fish are cooking, heat a third skillet over high heat and add 2 tablespoons of olive oil. Add the garlic and anchovies and stir constantly for a minute or so until the ingredients become fragrant. Remove from the heat and add the water, wine, clams, and chili flakes, then cover and return to the heat. Shake the pan from time to time until the shells have opened and the clams are cooked, about 5 minutes. Discard any clams that don't open and sprinkle the mixture with parsley.

Divide the potatoes and leeks among four bowls and drizzle with olive oil. Distribute the clams and broth among the bowls and top each with a fish fillet. Garnish with a squeeze of fresh lemon juice and serve immediately.

∞ **Note:** *If Manila clams are unavailable, you may substitute long neck clams, but because they are larger, you may wish to remove the cooked clams from the shells before serving.*

Blueberry sauce

2 cups chicken stock

¼ medium yellow onion, do not chop

¼ apple (Fuji or other sweet variety), do not chop

3 to 4 sprigs fresh thyme

2 cups fresh or frozen blueberries

1 ½ teaspoons freshly squeezed lemon juice

¼ teaspoon kosher salt

¼ teaspoon pepper

3 tablespoons unsalted butter, cut into ½-inch pieces

Salmon

1 (2-pound) salmon fillet, skinned and pin bones removed

4 tablespoons unsalted butter, melted

1 teaspoon capers, drained and mashed

1 teaspoon grated lemon zest

½ teaspoon garlic powder

½ teaspoon dried Italian herb blend

1 tablespoon minced yellow onion

½ teaspoon kosher salt

¼ teaspoon freshly ground black pepper

Serves 6

Butter-Rubbed Salmon with Blueberry Sauce

BENNETT'S, MERCER ISLAND
CHEF AND OWNER KURT DAMMEIER

The savory berry flavor of the sauce pairs beautifully with the salmon in this flavorful dish, but could also be used with grilled chicken or roast pork.

For the blueberry sauce:
Add the chicken stock to a small saucepan and bring to a boil. Reduce the heat to medium and add the onion, apple, and thyme. Simmer until the stock is reduced in half, about 30 minutes, stirring occasionally. Use a slotted spoon to remove the onion, apple, and thyme from the stock and discard.

Add the blueberries, raise the heat, and bring to a boil. Reduce the heat to medium–low and simmer, uncovered, until the liquid is reduced to ¾ cup, about 20 minutes. Remove the pan from the heat and stir in the lemon juice, salt, and pepper. Add the butter and whisk the sauce until the butter is completely melted, about 1 minute. Serve hot.

For the salmon:
Cut the salmon fillet at a 45–degree angle along the bias into 6 pieces, taking care to cut narrower slices from the thicker portion of the fillet and wider slices from the thinner portion.

Whisk together the butter, capers, lemon zest, garlic powder, Italian herbs, onion, salt, and pepper. Use a basting brush to coat one side of the salmon pieces with half of the rub. Refrigerate the salmon just until the butter hardens into a glaze, about 5 minutes.

In a large skillet over medium–high heat, lay the salmon pieces buttered side down and cook until the bottom half of the flesh is opaque, 2 to 3 minutes. Brush the remaining butter rub over the salmon and flip the pieces. Cook until the salmon is nearly opaque throughout, but still moist, about 1 more minute. Serve hot, topped with blueberry sauce.

Buttermilk Fried Quail with Asparagus Remoulade

WHITEHOUSE-CRAWFORD RESTAURANT, WALLA WALLA
CHEF JAMIE GUERIN

Whitehouse-Crawford is a favorite among visitors to the Walla Walla wine country, and has been called one of America's great rural restaurants. Chef Guerin combines the sophistication of quail with the comfort of fried chicken in this unusual entrée.

2 cups buttermilk

1 tablespoon Herbes de Provence

4 semi-boneless quail or Cornish game hens *(see Note)*

2 pounds asparagus, tough ends removed

½ cup mayonnaise

¼ cup whole grain mustard

Pepper

Peanut oil, for frying (about 1½ quarts) *(see Note)*

2 cups flour (or more as needed)

Salt and pepper

Honey, for garnish

Serves 4

Mix the buttermilk and herbs in a wide bowl. Completely submerge the quail in the buttermilk and refrigerate for at least 2 hours or up to overnight.

Shave the asparagus into thin ribbons with a vegetable peeler and place in a bowl. Add the mayonnaise and mustard and stir together; season with pepper to taste.

Add peanut oil to a depth of 3 to 4 inches in a large stockpot over medium-high heat. Season the flour with salt and pepper. Remove the quail from the buttermilk and dredge in the seasoned flour, shaking off any excess. Fry the quail one at a time until golden brown and cooked through, about 5 to 10 minutes. Drain on paper towels, sprinkle with salt while still very hot, and hold in a warm oven while you finish cooking the remaining quail.

Divide the asparagus mixture evenly among four plates and top each with a fried quail. Drizzle quail with honey and serve.

Note: *If you don't have access to quail, you can easily substitute small Cornish game hens in this recipe. Use kitchen shears to cut along either side of the spine to remove the back of the bird, and then carefully trim remaining ribs from the inside; you'll be left with a semi-boneless hen. If you prefer, simply ask your butcher to prepare the birds for you. Because the birds are deep fried in this recipe, you will need quite a bit of oil. If you don't have enough peanut oil, you may use half peanut oil and half canola oil.*

Elk ragu

2 pounds elk heart, cleaned
    and diced *(see Note on
    page 108)*

2 pounds elk meat (loin, shank,
    or shoulder), diced

12 ounces slab bacon, diced

1 Walla Walla sweet onion, diced

1 fennel bulb, trimmed and diced

3 medium carrots, peeled
    and diced

1 celery heart, leaves and
    core included, diced

1 tablespoon whole fennel seed

1 tablespoon brown mustard seed

2 teaspoons pepper

1½ tablespoons salt

1½ tablespoons sugar

1 teaspoon celery seed

1 cup rendered pork fat
    or canola oil

4 cups chicken stock

2 cups beef glacé
    (see Sources on page 174)

1 bottle red wine, reduced to 1 cup

(continued on page 108)

Cavatelli Cacciatore

ALTURA, SEATTLE   ℝ   CHEF AND OWNER NATHAN LOCKWOOD

This rich elk ragu, perfect for hunters, is enhanced by mushrooms and huckleberries and is best refrigerated for a day or two before serving, allowing the flavors to meld a bit. If you don't have access to elk, you may substitute bison or beef. Chef Lockwood, who trained under Hubert Keller and worked in Michelin-starred restaurants prior to launching Altura, makes hazelnut cavatelli pasta from scratch to serve with this ragu.

For the elk ragu:

Combine the elk heart, elk meat, bacon, onion, fennel, carrot, celery, fennel seed, mustard seed, pepper, salt, sugar, and celery seed in a large bowl and mix well to combine; chill thoroughly in the refrigerator. Grind the seasoned meat and vegetables through the large holes of a food processor or a meat grinder.

Heat the pork fat in a large stockpot over medium-high heat and brown the ground meat and vegetables. When all the meat has been browned, add the chicken stock and scrape up any browned bits from the bottom of the pan. Add the glacé and the reduced red wine, bring to a boil, and then reduce the heat and simmer until thickened, about 30 minutes.

For the cavatelli cacciatore:

Bring a large pot of salted water to a boil. Add the cavatelli and cook until tender but still al dente, about 4 to 6 minutes for fresh pasta, or longer for dried pasta.

(continued on page 108)

Cavatelli cacciatore

1 pound cavatelli pasta
  or other short pasta

1 ½ pounds fresh porcini
  mushrooms, cleaned
  and diced (or equivalent
  of rehydrated dried porcini
  mushrooms)

4 tablespoons unsalted butter

4 cups fresh huckleberries
  or blueberries

Minced fresh sage leaves,
  for garnish

Serves 8 (with extra ragu)

While the pasta cooks, reheat 4 cups of the elk ragu over medium-high heat. Stir in the mushrooms until heated through, then remove from the heat and stir in the butter. Drain the pasta and add it to the ragu. Add the huckleberries, toss together, and serve immediately, garnished with sage leaves.

❧ *Note: This rich hunter's ragu is proportioned to use a single whole heart, resulting in a large batch of ragu, which can be frozen. If you don't have access to the heart, or don't wish to use it, you may substitute more elk meat, or use bison or beef instead.*

Chateaubriand

EL GAUCHO, SEATTLE
FOUNDER AND OWNER PAUL MACKAY
CORPORATE EXECUTIVE CHEF AND OWNER KEN SHARP

Just follow a few steakhouse secrets, like bathing your cooked steak in mustard-infused butter before serving and creating a robust cliff sauce for the steak, and you'll be on your way to preparing the perfect dinner for any special occasion. At El Gaucho, chateaubriand is served with grilled asparagus, crimini mushrooms, broiled tomatoes, and baked potatoes with cheddar cheese sauce.

1 thick center-cut filet mignon steak
(about 1 pound)

1 to 2 tablespoons Gaucho
or other steak seasoning
(see Sources on page 174)

2 tablespoons butter, melted

1 teaspoon Coleman's dry mustard

1 tablespoon butter

1 tablespoon flour

½ cup beef stock

1 teaspoon Worcestershire sauce

2 tablespoons Cabernet Sauvignon
wine

Serves 2

Preheat a charcoal or gas grill to medium *(see Note)*. Rub the filet mignon with the steak seasoning. Grill the filet mignon over medium heat until the internal temperature measures the desired level, approximately 20 minutes to reach 120 degrees for medium rare, turning every 3 to 4 minutes until done. Remove the meat to a cutting board to rest for a few minutes. While the meat is resting, combine the melted butter and dry mustard and pour over the cooked filet mignon.

To prepare the cliff sauce, combine the butter and flour in a small saucepan over medium–high heat and whisk together as the butter melts. Whisk in the stock and Worcestershire sauce and stir until bubbling and slightly thickened. Remove from the heat and stir in the wine.

Slice the filet mignon into 2 thick slices and divide between two plates. Pour any of the drippings from the resting meat into the cliff sauce, stir to combine, and pour the sauce over the sliced filet mignon to serve.

❧ **Note:** *You may also cook the filet mignon by heating an oven-safe sauté pan over high heat. Add 2 tablespoons of canola oil, sear the meat on all sides, and then transfer the entire pan to the oven to finish cooking to the desired internal temperature.*

1/4 cup extra virgin olive oil

8 large beef short ribs
(about 3 to 4 pounds)

Kosher salt and pepper

1 cup diced carrots

1 cup diced yellow onion

3/4 cup cherries (dried, fresh,
or frozen)

1/3 cup balsamic vinegar

1/2 cup Chateau Ste. Michelle Syrah
or other full-bodied red wine

2 tablespoons chili powder

1/2 cup brown sugar

1 tablespoon chipotle peppers
in adobo (about 2 peppers)

1 tablespoon dry oregano

1 tablespoon dry mustard

1/4 cup ketchup

1 cup beef stock

Serves 8

Cherry Chipotle Short Ribs

CHATEAU STE. MICHELLE, WOODINVILLE   CHEF JOHN SARICH

There is something magical about slow cooking short ribs. In this recipe, large, tough cuts of meat become a tender and succulent treat, thanks to several hours in a richly flavored sauce. For wine pairings, Chef Sarich suggests Chateau St. Michelle's Artist Series Meritage, Grenache Limited Release, or Cold Creek Vineyard Syrah.

Heat a large Dutch oven or heavy-bottomed saucepan over medium heat and add the olive oil. Season the short ribs with salt and pepper and brown on all sides. Remove the ribs and hold on a platter.

Add the carrots and onions and sauté until soft, about 5 minutes. Add the cherries, vinegar, wine, chili powder, brown sugar, peppers, oregano, mustard, ketchup, and beef stock and bring to a boil. Return the short ribs to the pan, nestling the ribs into the braising liquid. Cover, reduce the heat to simmer, and cook until the ribs are tender and falling off the bone, about 2 to 3 hours.

Remove the short ribs from the pan and keep warm; discard the bones and trim the large layers of fat from the ribs. Place the liquid from the pan into a blender and blend until smooth. Strain the sauce for a more finished sauce, or leave coarse for a rustic style. Season with salt and pepper to taste and serve the ribs with sauce poured over them.

Chicken Pot Pie

VOLUNTEER PARK CAFE, SEATTLE
CHEF AND OWNER ERICKA BURKE

Ericka Burke and the staff at VPC have an almost cult-like following. They celebrate the fresh, local, and seasonal bounty of the Pacific Northwest with food that is simple and straightforward, just like this comforting Chicken Pot Pie.

½ pound puff pastry (1 sheet of frozen puff pastry dough)

¼ cup extra virgin olive oil

3 large carrots, peeled and diced small

6 celery stalks, diced small

1 small yellow onion, diced small

8 small red potatoes, skin on, diced small

2 tablespoons minced fresh thyme

1 tablespoon minced lemon zest (about 1 lemon zested)

4 medium boneless chicken breast halves, diced

¼ cup dry white wine

1 cup chicken broth

3 cups heavy cream

½ cup (1 stick) unsalted butter

½ cup flour

½ cup fresh or frozen peas

½ cup fresh or frozen pearl onions

¼ cup chopped Italian parsley

Salt and pepper

1 egg

2 tablespoons milk

Serves 6

Roll out the puff pastry to ¼ inch on a lightly floured surface. Place six 12-ounce oven-safe baking dishes over the pastry dough and cut around the dishes with a knife. Place the pastry pieces on a sheet pan lined with parchment or a silicone liner and cut a small slit in the center of each pastry. Chill the pastry tops in the freezer for 20 minutes.

While the puff pastry is chilling, heat the oil in a large stockpot over medium-high heat. Add the carrots, celery, onion, and potatoes, reduce the heat to medium, and cook until tender, about 10 minutes, taking care not to brown the vegetables. Add the thyme and lemon zest, stir to combine, and then add the chicken. Continue cooking over medium heat until the chicken is cooked through, about 8 to 10 minutes. Add the white wine and chicken broth and stir to scrape any browned bits from the bottom of the pan. Reduce the liquid slightly, and then add the cream.

Melt the butter in a sauté pan over medium heat and whisk in the flour a little at a time until well mixed. Continue cooking until the roux is light golden brown, about 5 to 8 minutes. Slowly stir the roux into the chicken mixture until thickened. Add the peas and pearl onions and simmer for 5 minutes. Stir in the parsley and season with salt and pepper to taste. Cover and keep warm.

Preheat the oven to 350 degrees. Beat the egg and milk together to form an egg wash. Remove the puff pastry from the freezer and brush with the egg wash. Bake the puff pastry until golden brown, about 20 minutes.

To serve, fill the individual baking dishes with the hot chicken mixture and top with a circle of baked puff pastry. Serve hot.

Pickled apples

1 cup rice wine vinegar

¾ cup sugar

2 tablespoons salt

½ vanilla bean

1 sprig thyme

4 tart, firm apples,
   such as Granny Smith

Glaze

½ cup honey

½ cup pear vinegar
   or white wine vinegar

2 cups hard apple cider

2 pieces star anise

1 bay leaf

1 medium shallot, minced

2 tablespoons chopped pickled
   ginger

1 tablespoon Dijon mustard

Pork chops

2 tablespoons canola oil

4 pork chops

Salt and pepper

4 tablespoons cold unsalted butter

Fresh chopped chives, for garnish

Serves 4

Cider-Glazed Pork Chops with Pickled Apples

CHEF AND WRITER LISA NAKAMURA

Apples and pork are a classic flavor combination, but in this recipe Chef Nakamura has created an interesting play on sweet and sour flavors in the glaze and the pickled apples, both of which may be made ahead to save time.

For the pickled apples:
Combine the vinegar, sugar, and salt in a medium non-reactive stockpot over medium-high heat and bring to a boil. Stir until all of the sugar is dissolved. Remove from the heat, add the vanilla bean and thyme sprig, and cool to room temperature. Peel and core the apples, then cut into ¼-inch dice; add the apples to the pickling liquid and let the apples marinate in the refrigerator overnight. Unused pickled apples will hold for 1 to 2 weeks in the refrigerator.

For the glaze:
Heat a medium saucepan over high heat and cook the honey until it browns lightly, about 3 minutes. Add the vinegar, cider, star anise, bay leaf, and shallot and cook until the mixture is reduced by two-thirds. Remove the star anise and bay leaf and add the pickled ginger. Remove from the heat and whisk in the Dijon mustard. The glaze may be stored in an airtight container in the refrigerator for up to a week.

For the pork chops:
Heat a large skillet or sauté pan over high heat and add the canola oil. Season the pork chops with salt and pepper and cook them until medium, about 4 minutes per side. Remove the chops from the pan and keep warm. Drain off any excess oil from the pan, add the glaze, and cook until it becomes syrupy, about 2 minutes. Whisk the cold butter into the glaze, return the pork chops to the pan, and spoon the glaze over the pork chops to reheat them. Serve with fresh chopped chives and pickled apples for garnish.

Beans

1 pound dried white beans

4 quarts water

½ pound pork belly or thick-cut bacon, cut into ½-inch-thick slices

4 parsley sprigs

2 garlic cloves

¼ teaspoon dried thyme

2 bay leaves

½ tablespoon salt

Cassoulet

1½ pounds lamb (preferably shoulder meat), cut in chunks

3 tablespoons rendered duck fat or canola oil, divided

1 large onion, diced

2 large garlic cloves, minced

4 plum tomatoes, diced

½ tablespoon tomato paste

¼ teaspoon dried thyme, or 1 teaspoon fresh thyme

1 bay leaf

2 cups dry white wine

½ cup veal stock (see Note)

1½ cups chicken stock

Salt and pepper

Luc's Cassoulet

LUC, SEATTLE   CHEF THIERRY RAUTUREAU/CHEF IN THE HAT™

Don't be deterred by the long list of ingredients or the steps involved in making this classic cassoulet. The beans and meat can be prepared ahead of time, making assembly a snap, or prepare the entire dish ahead of time and simply bake the cassoulet when you're ready.

For the beans:

Wash and drain the beans and place them in a large pot; add the water, cover, and bring to a boil. Boil uncovered for 2 minutes, then cover, turn off the heat, and let soak for 1 hour.

When the beans have finished soaking, bring them to a simmer and add the pork belly, parsley, garlic, thyme, bay leaves, and salt. Simmer slowly, partially covered, until the beans are just tender, about 1 hour. Near the end of cooking, stir in the salt. Use a slotted spoon to remove the pork belly, parsley, and bay leaf, which will all float to the top. The beans may be cooked ahead and refrigerated until you are ready to assemble the cassoulet.

For the cassoulet:

Pat the lamb pieces dry with paper towels. Heat a large Dutch oven over medium–high heat and add 2 tablespoons of the duck fat. Heat to very hot, but not smoking, and brown the lamb pieces, a few at a time, removing them to a dish. Pour off any excess fat and return the pot to the heat; add the onions and cook until lightly browned.

Return the lamb to the pot and add the garlic, tomatoes, tomato paste, thyme, bay leaf, wine, veal stock, and chicken stock. Season lightly with salt, cover, and bring to a simmer. Cook slowly until the lamb is tender, about 1½ hours. Season with salt and pepper to taste and allow the lamb to cool. The lamb may be cooked ahead and refrigerated in its cooking liquid until you are ready to assemble the cassoulet.

¾ pound kielbasa or cooked
　　chorizo sausage, cut into chunks

¾ pound duck confit meat,
　　cut into chunks (about 4 legs,
　　skin and bones discarded)
　　(see Sources on page 174)

1 to 2 cups fresh breadcrumbs
　　(from white bread)

¼ cup minced fresh parsley

Serves 8

To assemble:

Preheat the oven to 325 degrees. Heat the remaining tablespoon of duck fat in a skillet over medium-high heat and lightly brown the kielbasa. If you prepared the lamb ahead, remove the lamb from the refrigerator and discard any surface fat.

Using a slotted spoon, remove the beans from their liquid. Arrange one-third of the beans in the bottom of one 6-quart casserole or two 3-quart casseroles. Combine the lamb, duck, and sausage, and layer half of the meat mixture over the beans. Repeat with a layer of beans, then a layer of meat, and end with a layer of beans. Ladle the lamb cooking liquid over the top just to cover the beans (the casserole will be very full). Spread the breadcrumbs and parsley over the top and cover.

Bake the covered casserole for 1 hour, and then remove the cover and bake until the breadcrumb topping is crusted and lightly browned, about 10 more minutes, adding more of the cooking liquid from the beans if the cassoulet seems too thick or the beans dry out. Let stand a few minutes before serving.

  ⊗ **Note:** *Veal stock adds richness and viscosity to the dish, but you may substitute beef or chicken stock if it's not available.*

Hot sauce

3 ounces tomato paste
  (½ (6-ounce) can)

2 chipotle peppers in adobo sauce

8 medium garlic cloves

½ cup chopped cilantro

2 cups apple cider

1 cup water

½ cup apple cider vinegar

1 tablespoon salt

¼ cup honey

½ cup brown sugar

Cucumber apple relish

1 Granny Smith apple, diced

1 English cucumber, seeded
  and diced

½ red bell pepper, diced

½ medium red onion, diced

1 small garlic clove, minced

½ bunch cilantro, chopped fine

1 small lime, zested and juiced

Salt and pepper

Northwest Fish Tacos

MAXWELL'S, TACOMA   ❧   CHEF HUDSON SLATER

These tacos have a distinctive Northwest flair to them thanks to the crisp and refreshing apple relish. For the best flavor, use the freshest fish possible and make the relish and hot sauce the day before. Leftover relish can be tossed into a salad or combined with guacamole for a snack.

For the hot sauce:

Combine the tomato paste, chipotle peppers, garlic, cilantro, cider, water, vinegar, salt, honey, and brown sugar in a saucepan. Cook over medium heat, stirring until the sugar has dissolved. Continue to cook the sauce until it starts to bubble, about 15 minutes.

Puree the mixture with a stick blender or carefully transfer to a traditional blender and puree. Return the mixture to the pot and cook over medium heat for 30 minutes. Cool before using and store in the refrigerator for up to a week.

For the cucumber apple relish:

Combine the apple, cucumber, pepper, onion, garlic, and cilantro in a medium bowl and toss together. Add the lime zest and juice, toss to coat the ingredients, and season with salt and pepper to taste. Refrigerate until ready to serve.

For the fish tacos:

Combine the olive oil and garlic in a wide, shallow baking dish. Add the fish, turning to coat on all sides with the oil. Marinate in the refrigerator for 30 minutes.

Heat a grill to medium heat or heat a nonstick grill pan or griddle over medium heat. Remove the fish from the marinade and season the fish with cumin, coriander, salt, and pepper. Grill or sear the fish until cooked through, about 3 minutes per side.

Fish tacos

¼ cup extra virgin olive oil

2 garlic cloves, minced

1 pound coho salmon, cut into
    8 (2-ounce) portions *(see Note)*

Ground cumin

Ground coriander

Salt and pepper

16 small white-corn tortillas

2 ripe avocados, sliced

Fresh chopped cilantro,
    for garnish

2 limes, cut into wedges,
    for garnish

Serves 4 (2 tacos each)

Remove the fish fillets to a warm platter and grill the tortillas for about 1 minute per side. Place 2 tortillas on top of each other for each taco, and then place a piece of fish in the center. Add avocado slices to one side of the fish and the relish to the other side. Garnish with cilantro and serve with lime wedges and hot sauce on the side for dipping.

❧ **Note:** *Salmon, halibut, mahi mahi, ahi, albacore tuna, and corvina also work well in these tacos.*

Octopus

2½ pounds octopus (see Note)

½ cup extra virgin olive oil

1 bay leaf

2 garlic cloves, thinly sliced

½ cup dry white wine

Bolognese sauce

1 cup extra virgin olive oil

2 cups chopped yellow onion

4 garlic cloves, thinly sliced

1½ cups dry white wine

1 cup brandy

2 cups chopped tomatoes
      (see Note)

2 tablespoons chopped fresh
      savory or fresh thyme, divided

1 bay leaf

½ tablespoon chili flakes

2 tablespoons chopped parsley

1 lemon, zested and juiced

Serves 4 to 6

Octopus Bolognese

WESTWARD, SEATTLE ❧ CHEF ZOI ANTONITSAS

Chef Antonitsas first learned of octopus Bolognese from her mentor, Loretta Keller, who used to make a similar dish at Bizou. There it was stirred into risotto, drizzled with a garlicky aioli sauce, and topped with a grilled baby octopus and arugula leaves. The sauce is incredibly rich, and can also be served over pasta or spooned onto crostini for an appetizer. Because the octopus is very salty already, the Bolognese shouldn't require any additional salt.

For the octopus:
Preheat the oven to 375 degrees.

Combine the octopus, olive oil, bay leaf, garlic, and wine in a large, heavy-bottomed, oven-safe pot or Dutch oven. Turn the heat to medium and, when the octopus starts to sizzle, move the octopus around a bit to prevent it from sticking. Cover and place the entire pot in the oven. Cook until the octopus is tender, but not mushy, about 1 to 1½ hours. The octopus will shrink to about half its original weight as it cooks. Allow the octopus to cool completely in any cooking liquid in the refrigerator for several hours or overnight.

For the Bolognese sauce:
Heat a heavy-bottomed, medium stockpot over medium heat and add the olive oil, onion, and garlic. Cook until the vegetables are lightly browned, about 5 to 10 minutes, stirring frequently. Add the wine and brandy and cook until reduced by half, about 15 minutes. Add the tomatoes, half of the savory, the bay leaf, and the chili flakes, then reduce the heat to low and cook for 20 minutes, stirring occasionally.

While the sauce is cooking, remove the octopus from the liquid and finely chop the octopus. Add the octopus to the tomato sauce, cover, and cook over low heat for 45 minutes. Add the remaining savory, parsley, lemon zest, and juice and stir together. Serve the Bolognese over pasta, stirred into risotto, or over crostini.

❧ **Note:** *To ease in the preparation of this dish, ask your fishmonger to remove the ink sack and beak from the octopus and the skin from the body and legs. Use fresh tomatoes if tomatoes are in season and you can get sweet, vine-ripened ones; otherwise use high-quality canned tomatoes.*

Venison

8 venison shanks
  (see Note on page 120)

Salt and pepper

Flour

4 tablespoons butter

¼ cup canola oil or extra virgin
  olive oil

1 large carrot, diced

1 large onion, diced

3 celery stalks, diced

2 garlic cloves, chopped

½ cup white wine

1 (14.5-ounce) can diced
  or crushed tomatoes

3 bay leaves

1 small bunch fresh thyme

6 to 7 cups chicken stock

Fingerling potatoes

8 cups rock salt *(see Headnote)*

2 pounds fingerling potatoes

Gremolata

1 tablespoon chopped parsley

1 tablespoon chopped garlic

1 tablespoon lemon zest

Serves 4

Ossobuco with Salt-Roasted Fingerling Potatoes

THE BAY CAFÉ, LOPEZ ISLAND ❧ CHEF AND OWNER TIM SHEA

At the Bay Café, Chef Shea makes this classic dish with venison, but you may use lamb shanks or veal shanks if venison is not available. If you don't have rock salt, you can simply toss the potatoes with some olive oil and roast them until tender, about 40 minutes.

For the venison:
Preheat the oven to 325 degrees. Pat the venison shanks dry with paper towels, season with salt and pepper, and dredge in flour.

Heat a large Dutch oven or other oven-safe, heavy-bottomed pot (at least 6 inches deep) over high heat and add the butter and oil. When melted and hot, add the venison shanks a few at a time and brown on all sides. Remove from the pot and repeat with the remaining shanks.

When the shanks are all browned, add the carrot, onion, and celery to the pan, reduce the heat to medium-high, and sauté until translucent, about 5 minutes. Add the garlic and sauté for 2 more minutes. Add the white wine, stirring to pull up any browned bits from the bottom of the pan. Place the shanks on top of the vegetables, and then add the tomatoes, bay leaves, and thyme. Add enough chicken stock to cover the shanks, cover the pot, place in the oven, and cook until the meat falls from the bones, about 3 hours.

For the fingerling potatoes:
Preheat the oven to 450 degrees *(see Note on page 120)*. Fill the bottom of a 4-inch-deep roasting pan with half of the rock salt. Place the whole fingerling potatoes on top and cover with the remaining rock salt. Roast in the oven until tender, about 45 minutes to an hour.

(continued on page 120)

For the gremolata:

While the potatoes are cooking, combine the parsley, garlic, and lemon zest in a small covered container and refrigerate until ready to serve.

To assemble:

Use a slotted spoon to carefully remove the shanks to a warm plate. Place the pot over medium-high heat on the stove and simmer until the braising liquid is reduced by half, about 10 minutes. Strain the braising liquid and discard the solids.

Place the roasted fingerling potatoes on a large platter and top with the shanks. Pour the braising liquid over the shanks and garnish with the gremolata.

❧ *Note: Serve each person one large (hind) shank and one small (fore) shank to balance the servings. If you have only one oven, you may roast the potatoes in the oven with the lamb during the last hour of cooking.*

Cauliflower couscous

1 head cauliflower, chopped
    very small

1 tablespoon curry powder

1 teaspoon salt

¼ cup extra virgin olive oil

2 cups cooked Israeli couscous
    (about 1 cup dry)

Salt and pepper

Tomato-caper relish

½ cup diced grape tomatoes

1 tablespoon capers, drained
    and rinsed

1 teaspoon minced shallot

¼ cup extra virgin olive oil

Salt and pepper

Halibut

2 to 3 tablespoons clarified
    butter or olive oil

4 (6-ounce) halibut fillets
    (see Note on page 122)

Salt and pepper

1 tablespoon minced shallot

¼ cup white wine

(continued on page 122)

Pan Seared Halibut with Curry Roasted Cauliflower Couscous, Tomato-Caper Relish, and Arugula Beurre Blanc

FRASER'S GOURMET HIDEAWAY, OAK HARBOR, WHIDBEY ISLAND
CHEF AND OWNER SCOTT FRASER

Scott Fraser and his wife have been running Fraser's, a tucked-away jewel of a restaurant on Whidbey Island, since 2006. While a nice complement to the halibut, the cauliflower couscous in this recipe is an interesting side dish that would also pair well with meats or other seafood.

For the cauliflower couscous:
Preheat the oven to 400 degrees.

Toss the chopped cauliflower with the curry, salt, and olive oil and roast on a baking sheet until tender and lightly browned, about 20 minutes. Combine the cauliflower with the cooked couscous and season with salt and pepper to taste.

For the tomato-caper relish:
Combine the tomatoes, capers, shallot, and olive oil in a small bowl and season with salt and pepper to taste.

For the halibut:
Heat the clarified butter in a large skillet over medium–high heat. Season the halibut with salt and pepper and pan sear until lightly browned on each side and just barely cooked through, about 3 minutes per side, depending on thickness of the fillets. Remove to a warm plate and cover loosely with foil to keep warm.

(continued on page 122)

¼ cup fish stock or chicken stock

2 tablespoons heavy cream

4 tablespoons cold butter,
    cut into cubes

¼ cup arugula pesto (see Note)

Serves 4

Pour off any excess grease from the pan and return the pan to medium-high heat. Add the shallot and wine, stirring to pick up any browned bits from the pan. Reduce the wine by half, and then add the fish stock and cream and bring to a simmer. Reduce until slightly thickened, about 2 minutes, and then whisk in the butter a few cubes at a time. Remove the pan from the heat, whisk in the arugula pesto, and season with salt and pepper to taste.

Presentation:
Spoon the couscous onto four plates. Top each serving of couscous with a halibut fillet and spoon tomato-caper relish on top of the fish. Spoon the arugula beurre blanc over the fish and the couscous. Serve immediately.

❧ ***Note:*** *Chef Fraser prefers halibut fillets with the skin on, which helps to hold the fillet together while it cooks. If you use fillets with the skin on, cook them on the skin side until the skin is crispy, about 4 to 5 minutes, and then turn the fillets and cook for just 1 more minute on the second side. To make the arugula pesto, fill the bowl of a food processor with arugula leaves and, with the motor running, drizzle in olive oil until a paste forms, and then season with salt and pepper to taste. Extra pesto may be frozen for later use.*

Ginger-sake beurre blanc

¼ cup unsweetened rice vinegar

¾ cup sake

1 cup (2 sticks) cold, unsalted butter, cut into pieces

1 tablespoon finely chopped fresh ginger

½ teaspoon lemon zest

½ teaspoon salt

Sesame scallion rice cakes

2 cups sushi rice, rinsed several times

3 cups water

⅓ cup seasoned rice vinegar

1 whole egg, lightly beaten

¼ cup finely sliced green onions or chives

2 tablespoons toasted sesame seeds

Canola oil, for cooking

Scallops

24 scallops, cleaned of any side muscle and rinsed well

Salt

Canola oil, for cooking

Choppen green onions, for garnish

Serves 8

Pan Seared Sea Scallops on Sesame Scallion Rice Cakes with Ginger-Sake Beurre Blanc

BACKDOOR KITCHEN, FRIDAY HARBOR, SAN JUAN ISLAND
CHEFS AND OWNERS LEE AND SASHA HILDERMAN

The Hildermans serve this Asian-inspired entrée with a variety of local seasonal vegetables at their laid-back restaurant on San Juan Island.

For the ginger-sake beurre blanc:
Combine the rice vinegar and sake in a small saucepan over medium-high heat and bring to a boil. Reduce the mixture by three-quarters, reduce the heat to low, and whisk in the cold butter just until melted, taking care not to allow the sauce to become too hot and break. Remove from the heat and stir in the ginger, lemon zest, and salt. Keep warm until ready to serve.

For the sesame scallion rice cakes:
Combine the rice and water in a rice cooker and cook according to the manufacturer's directions. Spoon the cooked rice into a bowl and toss with the rice vinegar; set the bowl over an ice bath to cool the rice so you can handle it.

When the rice has cooled, add the egg, green onions, and sesame seeds and stir to combine. Scoop the seasoned rice onto a baking sheet or large cutting board into 8 equal portions. Wet your hands and form the portioned rice into ¾-inch-thick rice cakes.

Preheat a large skillet over medium heat and coat the bottom liberally with canola oil. Cook the rice cakes 3 at a time until golden brown, crispy, and hot through the middle, about 5 minutes per side. Hold on a warm platter until all of the rice cakes are cooked.

(continued on page 124)

For the scallops:

Pat the scallops dry and season with salt. Heat a thin layer of oil in a skillet over high heat just until smoking. Working in batches so you don't crowd the scallops, sear the scallops until golden brown on both sides, about 2 minutes per side. Remove to a warm plate to hold and repeat with the remaining scallops, adding more oil as needed.

Presentation:

Arrange 3 scallops on top of each rice cake and drizzle with ginger-sake beurre blanc sauce. Garnish with chopped green onions.

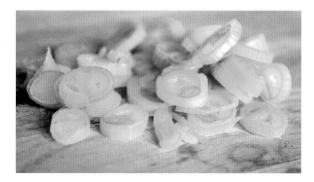

3 tablespoons brown sugar

2 tablespoons ground dry mustard

2 tablespoons onion powder

2 tablespoons garlic powder

2 tablespoons salt

2 tablespoons ground coriander

2 tablespoons white pepper

3 tablespoons smoked paprika

1 tablespoon pepper

4 boneless chicken breasts,
    skin on

8 slices thick-cut rye bread

Russian salad dressing, for serving

Lettuce leaves, for serving

Serves 4

Pastrami Roasted Chicken Sandwich

LLOYDMARTIN, SEATTLE   ❧   CHEF AND OWNER SAM CRANNELL

Chef Crannell cleverly mimics the flavor of pastrami in roast chicken with this flavorful spice blend. Although his recipe is showcased in a sandwich here, you can also use the rub to roast a whole chicken or chicken pieces for an entrée. Store leftovers of the spice mixture in a covered container in the pantry.

Preheat the oven to 350 degrees.

Combine the brown sugar with the mustard, onion powder, garlic powder, salt, coriander, white pepper, paprika, and pepper and stir together. Rub the chicken breasts liberally with the spice mixture and place on a rack over a rimmed baking sheet. Roast until the juices run clear from the meat, about 20 to 30 minutes, and then rest the chicken for 15 minutes.

After resting, thinly slice the chicken. Spread salad dressing on 4 of the bread slices and top each with a sliced chicken breast. Top with lettuce leaves and the remaining bread slices. Serve the sandwiches deli-style with a side of coleslaw.

Pepper and Goat Cheese-Filled Chicken Breasts

CHRISTOPHER'S ON WHIDBEY, COUPEVILLE, WHIDBEY ISLAND
CHEF AND PARTNER ANDREAS WURZRAINER

Chef Wurzrainer serves these stuffed chicken breasts over Mushroom Risotto (see recipe on page 68). To do the same, start the risotto in the same pan in which you sear the chicken to capture the wonderful flavors left behind in the pan.

1 large red pepper, diced

2 tablespoons extra virgin
olive oil, divided

Kosher salt and pepper

4 ounces goat cheese

8 very large basil leaves

4 "airline" chicken breasts
(see Note)

Serves 4

Preheat the oven to 375 degrees. Toss the diced peppers with 1 tablespoon of the olive oil and season with salt and pepper. Spread the peppers on a baking sheet and roast for 10 to 15 minutes.

Divide the goat cheese into 4 equal pieces and press into logs about 3 inches long. Lay 2 basil leaves flat next to each other, top with 1 of the pieces of goat cheese, and roll into a log with the basil on the outside. Repeat with the remaining basil leaves and goat cheese. The basil leaves will keep the cheese from oozing out of the chicken as it bakes, so make sure that the cheese is fully wrapped in the basil.

Lay the chicken breasts skin side up on a kitchen towel so they can't slide, and cut a pocket into the side of each breast about 2 inches long and as deep as the breast will allow without cutting through the breast.

Divide the roasted peppers evenly among the 4 breasts, tucking the peppers into the pockets. Stuff one of the basil and goat cheese logs into each breast, making sure the filling is pressed into the pockets as far as possible. Season both sides of the chicken breasts with salt and pepper.

Heat the remaining tablespoon of olive oil in a skillet over medium-high heat and sear 2 of the chicken breasts to a nice golden color on both sides. Transfer the chicken to a sheet pan, skin side down, and repeat with the remaining 2 breasts. Bake the breasts until they are cooked through, about 15 to 18 minutes, depending on thickness of the chicken.

❧ **Note:** *An "airline" breast refers to a chicken breast that has been deboned with the skin left on and the wing, with the bone intact, still attached.*

1 strip of bacon, diced

½ cup finely chopped yellow onion

¼ cup minced green onions

2 tablespoons chopped garlic

½ cup finely chopped celery

2 tablespoons butter

1 cup thinly sliced Yukon Gold
    potatoes

2 pounds fresh Manila clams,
    washed

1 cup vegetable stock

1 cup heavy cream

1 teaspoon cracked pink
    peppercorns

2 tablespoons chopped jalapeño
    (about 1 large or 2 small)

¼ cup chopped parsley

2 limes, zested

24-inch sprig fresh pine or spruce,
    broken into a couple pieces

4 (5- to 6-ounce) salmon fillets

Kosher salt

Serves 4

Pine and Spruce Smoked Salmon with Clam, Parsley, and Lime Chowder

CRUSH, SEATTLE   ❧   CHEF JASON WILSON

This simple smoking technique yields incredibly tender and juicy salmon with a unique smoky flavor that is complemented nicely by the chowder.

Heat a large sauté pan over medium–high heat. Add the bacon, onion, green onions, garlic, celery, and butter and cook until fragrant, about 4 minutes. Add the potatoes, clams, stock, and cream and simmer for another 6 minutes.

Strain the mixture and reserve both the solids and the cooking liquid for the chowder. Combine the cooking liquid with the pink pepper-corns, jalapeño, parsley, and lime zest and puree to create a smooth, green chowder. Combine the cooked vegetables and clams with the chowder liquid and keep warm until ready to serve.

Line a large sauté pan with foil and place the pine and spruce pieces in the pan over high heat. Cover the pan and cook until the needles and twigs begin to smoke, about 5 to 10 minutes. Spray a piece of aluminum foil with cooking spray and lay it on top of the needles and twigs. Place the salmon on the foil, seal the pan tightly with another piece of aluminum foil, cover, reduce heat to medium, and cook until the salmon is done, about 10 minutes.

To serve, ladle the chowder into the bottom of four wide soup bowls and place the salmon fillets on top.

Pork

1 pork loin roast (about 1½ to 2 pounds)

Salt and pepper

2 tablespoons extra virgin olive oil

Balsamic cherry sauce

1 cup fresh or frozen cherries, pitted and quartered

1 teaspoon butter

½ cup aged balsamic vinegar

Artichokes

2 tablespoons extra virgin olive oil

16 baby artichokes, cleaned, cut in half, and blanched (on page 130)

¼ cup toasted pistachio nuts

1 tablespoon chopped parsley

1 tablespoon chopped mint

Salt and pepper

Serves 4

Pork Chuck Loin with Artichokes, Pistachios, and Balsamic Cherry Sauce

STAPLE & FANCY MERCANTILE, SEATTLE
CHEF ETHAN STOWELL

For this roast, Chef Stowell prefers the chuck portion of the loin—the tip where the loin meets the shoulder—but you can use a boneless shoulder roast, a small pork loin, or even two small pork tenderloins. Different cuts will cook differently, so be sure to monitor the internal temperature of the meat while it's roasting.

For the pork:
Preheat the oven to 350 degrees.

Season the pork with salt and pepper. Heat a large, oven-safe skillet over medium-high heat and add the olive oil. Brown the pork on all sides, about 3 to 4 minutes per side. When the pork is browned, place the pan in the oven and roast until the center of the loin measures 140 degrees on an instant-read thermometer.

Remove the pork from the oven and place on a wire rack. Loosely tent with foil and allow the pork to rest for at least 15 to 20 minutes before slicing.

For the balsamic cherry sauce:
While the pork is resting, place a medium sauté pan over medium heat and sauté the cherries in the butter for 2 to 3 minutes. Add the balsamic vinegar and cook until the vinegar has reduced and thickened, about 10 to 15 minutes. Cover and keep warm until you are ready to serve.

(continued on page 130)

For the artichokes:

Add the olive oil to a medium sauté pan over medium–high heat and add the artichokes. Cook until the artichokes are heated all the way through, stirring occasionally, about 5 minutes *(see Note)*. Stir in the pistachios, parsley, and mint and season with salt and pepper to taste.

To assemble:

Divide the artichokes and pistachios among four warm plates. Slice the pork and lay the pork slices on top of the artichokes. Spoon the sauce over the pork slices and serve immediately.

❧ **Note:** *Baby artichokes can be difficult to find in some areas and during some seasons, so you may substitute two 14-ounce cans of artichoke hearts instead. Simply drain them and cut in half, heat them in a small sauté pan, and then combine with the other ingredients.*

2 tablespoons butter

1 tablespoon extra virgin olive oil

¼ pound bacon, cut into ½-inch
    pieces (about 4 thick slices)

2 pounds bone-in chicken pieces
    (4 breast halves or 4 whole legs)

Kosher salt

Pepper

Freshly ground nutmeg

2 medium onions, chopped

4 medium garlic cloves, thinly sliced

½ pound mushrooms, thinly sliced

1 bottle Riesling wine

1 cup heavy cream

3 tablespoons chopped parsley

Serves 4

Poulet au Riesling
(Chicken with White Wine)

RESTAURANT MARCHÉ, BAINBRIDGE ISLAND
CHEF AND OWNER GREG ATKINSON

Made with white wine instead of the traditional red, this dish bears some allegiance to coq au vin, but comes together far more quickly and has a fresher and lighter taste. Instead of the usual button mushrooms, Chef Atkinson uses forest mushrooms like chanterelles, shiitake, or morels, and he is adamant about using free-range, organic chicken.

Heat a large, heavy-bottomed stockpot or Dutch oven over medium-high heat and add the butter and oil. When the butter has melted, add the bacon and cook until crisp. Remove the bacon bits using a slotted spoon and set aside.

Season the chicken pieces with salt, pepper, and nutmeg, arrange them in the pot, skin side down, and brown on both sides. When browned, remove the chicken and set aside. Pour off and discard all but 3 to 4 tablespoons of the fat and reduce the heat to medium. Add the onions and garlic and sauté, stirring occasionally, until the onions have softened but not colored, about 5 minutes.

Add the mushrooms and cook until they are heated through, about 3 minutes. Raise the heat to high, add the wine, and bring to a boil. Return the chicken to the pot and reduce the heat to medium-low. Simmer, uncovered, until the chicken is cooked through, about 30 to 45 minutes.

Remove the chicken pieces from the pot and hold on a warm plate. Add the cream and boil until the sauce is reduced somewhat and beginning to thicken, about 5 minutes. Return the chicken to the pot along with any juices that have accumulated. Sprinkle with chopped parsley and the reserved bacon and serve with buttered noodles.

Pickled pepper relish

1 cup white wine

1 cup white vinegar

1 teaspoon salt

½ teaspoon pepper

1 teaspoon cumin

1 teaspoon coriander

2 garlic cloves, sliced

4 jalapeños, sliced in half lengthwise, seeds and ribs removed

3 Roma tomatoes, seeded and diced small

1 small yellow onion, diced small

Chèvre aioli

2 eggs

1 teaspoon Dijon mustard

2 tablespoons freshly squeezed lemon juice

2 garlic cloves, minced

Pinch cayenne pepper

½ teaspoon salt

¼ teaspoon pepper

½ cup canola oil

½ cup extra virgin olive oil

2 ounces crumbled goat cheese

Prima Lamb Burger with Pickled Pepper Relish and Chèvre Aioli

PRIMA BISTRO, LANGLEY, WHIDBEY ISLAND
CHEF AND OWNER SIEB JURRIAANS

The combination of seasoned lamb with the chèvre aioli and pickled pepper relish in this burger is both unique and irresistible. Make the relish and aioli the day before you plan to serve the burgers.

For the pickled pepper relish:
Combine the white wine, vinegar, salt, pepper, cumin, coriander, and garlic in a small sauté pan and bring to a boil. Add the jalapeños, cover, reduce the heat, and simmer for 20 minutes.

Remove the jalapeños and reserve the pickling liquid. When cool enough to handle, mince the jalapeños and toss together with the tomatoes and onions. Place all of the vegetables in a quart-size mason jar and pour the pickling mixture over the top. Refrigerate for at least 1 day and up to a week.

For the chèvre aioli:
Combine the eggs, mustard, lemon juice, garlic, cayenne, salt, and pepper in a blender. Turn the blender on and slowly pour in the canola oil and olive oil in a steady stream until thick and incorporated. Spoon into a covered container and stir in the goat cheese; refrigerate until ready to use.

Lamb burgers

1 ⅓ pound ground lamb

1 large shallot, chopped

3 garlic cloves, minced

1 to 2 tablespoons minced
fresh rosemary

Salt and pepper

4 brioche buns or other bun
of your choice

Arugula, for garnish

Serves 4

For the lamb burgers:

Heat the grill to medium–high heat. Gently mix the lamb with the shallot, garlic, and rosemary and form into 4 patties, taking care not to overwork the meat. Season each patty with salt and pepper and grill the patties to medium rare, about 3 minutes per side. Remove the patties from the grill and let rest while you toast the buns.

To assemble:

Spread chèvre aioli on both sides of the buns. Serve the burgers with arugula and a heaping tablespoon of the pickled pepper relish.

Ginger carrot coulis

2 tablespoons extra virgin olive oil

1 pound carrots, peeled and chopped

1 to 2 tablespoons chopped fresh ginger

¼ cup chopped sweet onion

2 tablespoons chopped garlic

1 large leek, white part only, chopped

½ cup chopped parsley

¼ teaspoon ground fennel seed

¼ teaspoon red chili flakes

1 teaspoon salt

½ teaspoon ground white pepper

½ teaspoon ground cumin

½ teaspoon ground coriander

1 cup dry white wine

1 cup water

2 tablespoons lime juice

1 cup carrot juice

Risotto

1 tablespoon unsalted butter

1 tablespoon extra virgin olive oil

(continued on page 136)

Prosciutto-Wrapped Halibut with Sweet Pea Risotto and Ginger Carrot Coulis

MAXWELL'S, TACOMA   ❧   CHEF HUDSON SLATER

This dish represents Chef Slater's nod to the classic combination of peas and carrots, and the risotto complements the halibut perfectly. Stir a little stock or cream into any leftover coulis for an easy and flavorful carrot soup.

For the ginger carrot coulis:

Heat the olive oil in a large stockpot over medium heat. Add the carrots, ginger, onion, garlic, leek, parsley, fennel, chili flakes, salt, pepper, cumin, and coriander and sauté for 5 minutes, taking care not to brown the vegetables.

Add the white wine, water, lime juice, and carrot juice and cook over low to medium heat until the carrots are soft, stirring occasionally and taking care not to burn the bottom of the pan, about 30 minutes.

When the carrots are soft, puree with a stick blender or working in batches in a traditional blender. Thin with a little water if the mixture is too thick. Set aside and rewarm as needed just before serving. The coulis may be made the day before and refrigerated.

For the risotto:

Heat the butter and olive oil in a large saucepan over medium heat. Add the onion and garlic and sauté until translucent, about 3 to 4 minutes. While the vegetables are cooking, puree 1 cup of the peas in the blender and set aside.

Add the rice to the saucepan and stir until coated, then add the wine and stir until all of the liquid is absorbed. Add 1 cup of the broth and

(continued on page 136)

½ yellow onion, diced

1 garlic clove, diced

2 cups frozen peas, thawed, divided

2 cups Arborio rice

1 cup dry white wine

3 to 4 cups vegetable or chicken broth

½ cup heavy cream

¾ cup freshly grated Parmesan cheese

1 small red bell pepper, diced

Kosher salt and pepper

Chive flowers, thinly sliced basil, or microgreens, for garnish (optional)

Halibut

6 (6-ounce) halibut fillets, skinned and pin bones removed

Salt and pepper

6 thin slices prosciutto

2 tablespoons unsalted butter

Serves 6

cook until absorbed, stirring occasionally. Add the remaining broth, ½ cup at a time, stirring until each portion is absorbed before adding the next. Continue adding broth until the rice is cooked al dente, about 35 minutes; discard any unused broth. Remove from the heat and cover to keep warm.

For the halibut:
Season the halibut fillets with salt and pepper. Wrap each of the halibut fillets in a thin slice of prosciutto. Heat a large skillet over medium heat and add the butter to the pan. When the butter starts to turn a light brown, cook the halibut fillets until lightly browned on each side and cooked through, about 2 to 3 minutes per side.

To assemble:
Stir the heavy cream, Parmesan, bell pepper, and pureed peas into the risotto and season with salt and pepper to taste. Fold in the remaining whole peas.

Spoon the carrot coulis on one side of six large, warm plates. Spoon the risotto on the other half. Place the seared halibut on top of the risotto. Garnish with chive flowers, thinly sliced basil, or microgreens.

Chicken

1 (3- to 4-pound) roasting chicken

6 tablespoons unsalted butter
(see Note on page 138)

Sea salt and pepper

Mushrooms

8 ounces wild mushrooms
(such as morels or chanterelles)

2 tablespoons butter, divided

Salt and pepper

1 small leek, split, sliced,
and cleaned well

1 shallot, minced

1 garlic clove, minced

¼ cup Calvados

¼ cup white wine

1 cup heavy cream

1 sage leaf, finely chopped

Serves 2 to 4

Roast Chicken with Creamy Wild Mushrooms

LE PICHET, SEATTLE
EXECUTIVE CHEF AND CO-OWNER JIM DROHMAN

Poulet rôti et ses champignons du bois à la crème is nothing short of legendary on the menu at Le Pichet, where Chef Drohman recommends pairing the dish with a lighter Burgundy red wine. Cut the cream in half for slightly less decadent, but still quite creamy, mushrooms.

For the chicken:
Preheat the oven to 500 degrees. Truss the chicken. Using a heavy roasting pan just large enough to hold the bird, melt the butter in the roasting pan over medium heat. When the butter is foamy, place the bird in the pan, breast side up. Baste well with the butter and season liberally with salt and pepper.

Place the chicken in the oven and roast until the internal temperature reaches 165 degrees, about an hour, basting once or twice during the cooking.

For the mushrooms:
While the chicken is roasting, clean the mushrooms using a mushroom brush or dry towel and remove the woody ends of the mushroom stems.

Heat a sauté pan large enough to hold the mushrooms in a single layer over medium heat and add 1 tablespoon of butter. When the butter foams, add the mushrooms, season with salt and pepper, and sauté quickly. Add the leek, shallot, and garlic and sauté over medium heat until tender, but don't allow the vegetables to brown.

(continued on page 138)

Add the Calvados, stir, and reduce until dry. Add the white wine and reduce again until dry. Add the cream and chopped sage and bring to a boil. Reduce the heat and simmer until the sauce is just thick enough to coat the back of a spoon, about 5 minutes, and then season with salt and pepper to taste. Finish the sauce by whisking in the remaining tablespoon of butter and serve immediately with the roast chicken. (Remove the trussing string before serving.)

❧ *Note: If you prepare your chicken using melted butter for basting, be aware that your oven is likely to smoke quite a bit. To minimize the smoking, instead of butter, rub the chicken with olive oil before seasoning with salt and pepper, and baste with the chicken fat that is rendered while roasting.*

Yogurt sauce

1 cup Greek yogurt

2 cloves garlic, pasted

Lemon juice

Salt and pepper

Lamb

½ cup garlic cloves

1 tablespoon kosher salt

¼ teaspoon saffron

1 tablespoon finely chopped
  ginger

1 tablespoon chopped
  preserved lemon, peel only, no
  pith (see Sources on page 174)

1 cup ground ras el hanout
  (see Note on page 140)

1 leg of lamb, deboned

Fresh chopped cilantro, green
  onions, or mint, for garnish

Extra virgin olive oil, for garnish

Squash zaalouk

2 tablespoons extra virgin olive oil

4 garlic cloves, sliced

2 cups diced summer squash

(continued on page 140)

Roast Leg of Lamb with Squash Zaalouk and Yogurt Sauce

SAFFRON MEDITERRANEAN KITCHEN, WALLA WALLA
CHEF CHRIS AINSWORTH

Always fascinated with the flavors of North Africa and the Eastern Mediterranean, Chef Ainsworth reinterprets some of those flavors using the bounty of the Walla Walla Valley in this dish with pronounced Moroccan flavors. While the restaurant serves a unique green garbanzo bean bissara to accompany the lamb, hummus would pair equally well. For the best flavor, marinate the lamb the night before you plan to roast it.

For the yogurt sauce:
Combine the yogurt with the pasted garlic and add lemon juice to taste. Season with salt and pepper to taste and refrigerate until ready to use.

For the lamb:
Combine the garlic and salt in the bowl of a food processor and let the blade run until the garlic forms a paste. Add the saffron, ginger, and preserved lemon and continue whirling until smooth. Stir in the ras el hanout. Rub the leg of lamb thoroughly with the paste and refrigerate for a few hours or overnight.

Preheat the oven to 325 degrees. Wipe the excess rub from the lamb, place the lamb on a rack over a rimmed baking sheet, and roast until the internal temperature registers 130 to 135 degrees for medium rare. Remove from the oven, tent loosely with foil, and let stand 10 minutes before slicing.

For the squash zaalouk:
While the lamb is resting, heat a medium sauté pan over medium-high heat and add the olive oil. Add the garlic, sauté for a minute,

(continued on page 140)

¼ cup diced onion

1 (14-ounce) can diced tomatoes

2 teaspoons ground cumin

2 teaspoons harissa powder

Salt and pepper

Fresh lemon juice

Serves 6

and then add the squash and onion. Continue to sauté until the squash is slightly browned, about 5 minutes.

Add the tomatoes and bring to a simmer. Add the cumin and harissa powder and season with salt, pepper, and a little fresh lemon juice to your taste.

Presentation:
Slice the lamb and drizzle with the yogurt sauce. Serve with the squash and garnish with cilantro, green onions, or mint and a drizzle of extra virgin olive oil.

❧ ***Note:*** *Ras el hanout is a complex spice blend used frequently in Moroccan cooking. If you can't find the spice blend, you can easily make your own by combining 2 tablespoons each of ground cumin, ground ginger, turmeric, salt, sugar, pepper, cinnamon, and coriander with 1 tablespoon each of cayenne, nutmeg, ground fennel seeds, and ground cloves. Store extra spice mix in an airtight container in the pantry.*

3 tablespoons extra virgin olive oil

¼ cup brown sugar

1 teaspoon cinnamon

½ teaspoon nutmeg

Pinch ground cloves

Pinch allspice

1 tablespoon pepper

3 tablespoons salt

1 (6-bone) pork loin roast
    with the fat cap intact

Serves 6

Roast Rack of Pork

LLOYDMARTIN, SEATTLE   ✕   CHEF AND OWNER SAM CRANNELL

While cooking a large roast is sometimes intimidating to inexperienced cooks, this might actually be one of the easiest recipes in this book, requiring just a simple but delicious spice rub before roasting in the oven. The finished dish makes for a stunning presentation on any dinner table.

Preheat the oven to 400 degrees. Combine the olive oil with the brown sugar, cinnamon, nutmeg, cloves, allspice, pepper, and salt and rub over the pork roast.

Place the roast, fat cap up, on a wire rack on a backing sheet and roast for 15 minutes uncovered. Reduce the heat to 350 degrees, cover with aluminum foil, and continue to roast until the internal temperature reaches 140 degrees for medium well, about an hour. Allow the roast to rest for 15 minutes before carving. Pork pairs well with fruit, so consider serving the sliced pork roast with Farro and Fig Salad or Warm Cinnamon Applesauce (*see recipes on pages 58 and 79, respectively*).

Shrimp stock

Shrimp shells *(see Note)*

2 tablespoons unsalted butter

2 leeks or 1 large yellow onion,
    coarsely chopped

2 carrots, peeled and
    coarsely chopped

5 stalks celery, coarsely chopped

1 fennel bulb, coarsely chopped
    (optional)

½ cup white wine

1 lemon, juiced

2 bay leaves

Cold water

Salt

Étouffée

6 tablespoons unsalted butter

½ cup flour *(see Note)*

3 cups chopped yellow onions
    (about 2 large onions)

1 cup chopped red bell peppers
    (about 1 large pepper)

1 cup chopped poblano peppers
    (about 2 medium peppers)

1 cup chopped celery
    (about 2 stalks)

Shrimp Étouffée

WHOOPEMUP HOLLOW CAFÉ, WAITSBURG
HEAD CHEF BRYANT BADER AND PASTRY CHEF VALERIE MUDRY

Don't be put off by the long list of ingredients for this recipe, as it's actually quite easy to prepare quickly. If you have the time to make homemade shrimp stock, you'll definitely appreciate the flavor boost, but if not, you can use store-bought fish stock or chicken stock. Begin with smaller amounts of cayenne pepper, Creole seasoning, and hot sauce, adding more after tasting if you prefer additional heat.

For the shrimp stock:
Heat a large, heavy-bottomed stockpot over medium-high heat and melt the butter. Add the shrimp shells and cook for 3 minutes, stirring often. Add the leeks, carrots, celery, and fennel and cook for another 5 minutes, stirring often. Add the white wine, lemon juice, bay leaves, and just enough water to cover all of the ingredients and bring to a boil. Reduce the heat to medium and cook for 30 minutes. Strain the stock and discard the solids. Return the stock to the pot and simmer until reduced to 3 cups of stock. Season with salt to taste and refrigerate or freeze until you are ready to make the étouffée.

For the étouffée:
Heat a large, heavy-bottomed stockpot over medium heat and melt the butter. Reduce the heat to low, add the flour, and stir frequently for approximately 20 minutes to make a blonde roux, taking care not to burn the roux.

Add the onions, both peppers, celery, leeks, carrots, garlic, and fennel to the roux and cook for another 10 minutes, stirring often. Add the tomatoes, bacon, sausage, bay leaves, thyme, cayenne, Creole seasoning, and garlic sauce and cook for 3 more minutes. Add the stock, bring the mixture to a boil, reduce the heat to a simmer, and cook, uncovered, for 30 minutes, stirring occasionally.

1 cup finely chopped leeks
(about 1 medium leek)

½ cup minced carrots
(about 2 medium carrots)

2 tablespoons minced garlic
(about 4 cloves)

2 teaspoons ground fennel seeds

3 cups coarsely pureed tomatoes

½ pound bacon, cooked until crisp
and crumbled

½ pound cooked Andouille
sausage, sliced

4 bay leaves

1 tablespoon chopped fresh thyme

½ to 1 teaspoon cayenne pepper

1 to 2 tablespoons Creole seasoning

1 to 2 tablespoons garlic sauce
or hot sauce

3 cups shrimp stock or chicken stock

3 pounds shrimp, peeled and
deveined

½ cup chopped Italian parsley

Salt

4 cups cooked white rice
(2 cups dry)

½ cup sliced green onions

Serves 8

Add the shrimp and simmer for another 5 minutes, and then add the parsley and season with salt to taste. Serve immediately over rice and garnish with green onions.

❧ *Note: If you are making your own stock for this dish, buy unpeeled shrimp, use the peels to make the stock first, and then use the peeled and deveined shrimp in the étouffée. While a roux is traditionally used to thicken étouffée, this recipe can be made without it for those with gluten sensitivities. Simply reduce the final stew until it reaches the desired consistency.*

12 ounces spaghetti

2 tablespoons extra virgin olive oil,
   plus more for finishing

1 pint grape tomatoes, halved

6 cups baby arugula

Salt and pepper

8 ounces goat cheese, crumbled

¼ cup pine nuts, toasted

Serves 4

Spaghetti Ortolano

IL TERRAZZO CARMINE, SEATTLE
CHEF JUAN VEGA AND FOUNDER CARMINE SMERALDO

The late Carmine Smeraldo's reputation lives on at this upscale restaurant serving authentic Italian cuisine, and this quick and easy pasta dish is always popular with diners.

Cook the spaghetti according to the package directions until just al dente. Drain the pasta and reserve some of the pasta cooking water.

Heat 2 tablespoons of the olive oil in a large skillet over medium–high heat. Add the tomatoes and toss quickly in the hot oil just to heat through slightly. Add the arugula and the cooked pasta to the pan along with a little bit of the hot pasta water. Toss for a minute to slightly wilt the arugula and season with salt and pepper to taste.

Spoon the pasta onto a large serving platter and sprinkle with olive oil. Top with the crumbled goat cheese and toasted pine nuts and serve immediately.

Cashew cream sauce
(see Note on page 146)

1 cup cashews

2 cups water

1 teaspoon salt

1 tablespoon lemon juice

¼ teaspoon nutmeg

Ravioli

½ pound nettles or baby spinach
    or beet greens

¼ cup walnuts, toasted *(see Note)*

1 teaspoon extra virgin olive oil

½ yellow onion, diced small

1 garlic clove, minced

1 bunch kale, de-stemmed
    and roughly chopped

1 small lemon, zested

Salt and pepper

32 wonton wrappers
    (see Note on page 146)

3 teaspoons egg replacer mixed
    with 4 tablespoons water
    (see Note)

Radish salad

1 bunch radishes, very thinly sliced

(continued on page 146)

Spring Nettle Ravioli with Cream Sauce and Radish Salad

CAFÉ FLORA, SEATTLE   ∞   OWNER NAT STRATTON-CLARKE

Café Flora uses nettles, artichokes, and kale from local producers in this vegan ravioli with a cashew cream sauce. If you are allergic to nuts or you prefer a traditional cream sauce, see the Note below. Take care not to touch the nettles until they are blanched as they will sting, or use another green in their place.

For the cashew cream sauce:
Soak the cashews for 4 hours (or overnight) in room temperature water, making sure that the cashews are fully submerged.

Drain the cashews and reserve the soaking liquid. Place the soaked cashews, ¾ cup of the cashew soaking water, 2 cups water, salt, lemon juice, and nutmeg into the bowl of a food processor. Blend on high until smooth and creamy. If needed, add a bit more of the cashew soaking water until the sauce is truly creamy.

For the ravioli:
Bring 4 quarts of water to a boil and blanch the nettles for 30 seconds, taking care not to touch them before they are cooked. Drain and submerge the nettles in an ice bath until cooled, and then drain and pick off the woody stems. If you are using another type of green, wilt them and press out any excess water through a colander before proceeding.

Place the toasted walnuts in a food processor and pulse until finely chopped. Heat a large sauté pan over medium-high heat and add the olive oil. Add the onions and cook until they start to brown, about 5 minutes, then add the minced garlic and cook until aromatic, about 30 seconds more.

(continued on page 146)

½ pound Jerusalem artichokes
    or jicama, very thinly sliced

⅓ cup minced fresh chives

½ cup dried cranberries

1 small lemon, zested and juiced

1 teaspoon salt

½ teaspoon pepper

½ teaspoon nutmeg

1 bunch microgreens,
    for garnish (optional)

Serves 4

Add the nettles, kale, and lemon zest and cook for approximately 10 minutes. Place the filling in a food processor, pulse 6 to 8 times, season with salt and pepper to taste, stir in the walnuts, and let cool.

Place 16 wonton wrappers on a floured surface and place a heaping tablespoon of filling in the center of half of the wrappers. If you have extra filling, either add a bit more filling to each wrapper or freeze for another use. Use a pastry brush to brush the edges of the wrappers with the egg replacer mixture. Place another wrapper on top of the filling and run your finger along the edges to seal ravioli, pressing out any air as you seal the edges. Crimp edges with a ravioli wheel to fully seal. Repeat until you have 16 large ravioli.

For the radish salad:
Mix together the radishes, Jerusalem artichokes, chives, dried cranberries, lemon zest and juice, salt, pepper, and nutmeg in a small bowl and set aside.

To assemble:
Bring a large pasta pot full of salted water to a boil. Place the ravioli in boiling water for 3 minutes, working in batches so the pot isn't too crowded. While the ravioli cook, heat the cashew sauce in a small saucepan over low heat.

Gently remove the ravioli with a slotted spoon and place 4 ravioli on each of four plates. Cover the ravioli with the hot cashew cream sauce. Place ⅓ cup of radish and artichoke mixture in the center of the ravioli on each plate, top each with 1 tablespoon of the microgreens, and serve.

✎ *Note: If you are allergic to nuts, omit the nuts in the ravioli filling and substitute a traditional white sauce (or purchased Alfredo sauce) for the cashew cream sauce. For speed of assembly, this recipe uses wonton wrappers for the ravioli, but you may also make your own pasta dough if desired and cut it into ravioli after making sheets of pasta. The recipe calls for egg replacer to keep this recipe vegan, but if you aren't following a vegan diet you may use one egg beaten with a tablespoon of water to seal the edges of the ravioli.*

Thai stew base

3 cups chicken stock

6 thin slices of galangal
　　or fresh ginger

4 ounces lemongrass,
　　roughly chopped

1 ounce Kaffir lime leaves

1 tablespoon red curry paste
　　(or more if you like heat)

½ cup heavy cream

¼ cup fish sauce

¼ cup sugar

2 (14-ounce) cans coconut milk

Jasmine rice

1 cup Jasmine rice

1½ cups water

½ cup coconut milk

Thai seafood stew

½ cup (1 stick) clarified butter
　　or canola oil

4 (U/10 size) scallops

8 (16/20 size) prawns

16 Manila clams

16 mussels

(continued on page 148)

Thai Seafood Stew

AQUA BY EL GAUCHO, SEATTLE
CORPORATE EXECUTIVE CHEF AND OWNER KEN SHARP
AQUA BY EL GAUCHO EXECUTIVE CHEF STEVE CAIN

A hidden jewel perched at the tip of Pier 70 in Seattle, AQUA by El Gaucho is wrapped in walls of glass that showcase some of Seattle's finest views of Elliott Bay, Magnolia Bluff, and the Space Needle. This stew, with rich Thai flavors of lemongrass, ginger, and coconut, is a favorite at the restaurant.

For the Thai stew base:
Combine the chicken stock, galangal, lemongrass, and lime leaves in a large stockpot over medium-high heat and bring to a boil. Reduce the heat to low and add the red curry paste, cream, fish sauce, sugar, and coconut milk and simmer for 45 minutes. Strain and cool immediately. The base can be made up to 3 days ahead of time and stored in a covered container in the refrigerator.

For the jasmine rice:
Combine the jasmine rice, water, and coconut milk in a large stockpot over medium-high heat, cover, and bring to a boil. Reduce the heat and simmer until the water is absorbed, about 20 minutes. Remove from the heat and hold to keep warm until ready to serve.

For the Thai seafood stew:
Add the clarified butter to a large, deep sauté pan (at least 5 inches deep) and heat until it barely starts to smoke. Very gently add the scallops and prawns and sear the seafood on one side for about 1 minute. Turn the scallops and prawns over and add the clams and mussels along with the stew base; cover and bring to a boil.

As soon as the mixture is boiling, gently lay the white fish on top of the stew, cover the pot, reduce the heat to simmer, and cook until the clams and mussels open and the fish is cooked through, about 5 minutes. Add half of the basil and cilantro to the stew.

(continued on page 148)

½ pound firm white fish
  (such as halibut or cod)

½ cup sliced basil, divided

½ cup chopped cilantro, divided

Sesame seeds, for garnish
  (optional)

Serves 4

To *assemble*:

Place ½ cup of jasmine rice in each of four large, rimmed soup bowls and top each bowl with 4 clams, 4 mussels, 2 prawns, and 1 scallop. Divide the white fish among the bowls, ladle the sauce over the top, and garnish with the remaining basil and cilantro and the sesame seeds.

Desserts & Sweet Treats

Alsatian Apple Tart with Brown Butter Ice Cream, p. 151

½ cup (1 stick) butter, melted and cooled slightly

2 eggs, beaten

½ teaspoon vanilla extract

2 cups brown sugar

1½ cups flour

2 teaspoons baking powder

½ teaspoon salt

1 cup chopped pecans

16 Almond Roca toffees, crushed

Serves 16

Almond Roca Blondies

RUN OF THE RIVER INN & REFUGE, LEAVENWORTH
INNKEEPER JANNA BOLLINGER

Almond Roca butter crunch toffee, produced by the hundred-year-old Brown & Haley company in Tacoma, provides the perfect crunchy sweetness in these blondies.

Preheat the oven to 350 degrees. Spray a 13 x 9 x 2–inch baking dish with cooking spray.

Combine the melted butter with the eggs and vanilla in a mixing bowl and whisk together. Add the brown sugar, flour, baking powder, and salt and beat until smooth; fold in the pecans. Spread the batter into the prepared baking dish and bake until just set, about 30 to 45 minutes.

Remove the baking dish from the oven and sprinkle the crushed Almond Roca toffees over the top. Return the baking dish to the oven and continue baking until the blondies are cooked through and the top is gooey and golden, about 5 more minutes.

Ice cream

1 cup (2 sticks) butter

2 cups milk

2 cups heavy cream

8 egg yolks

1 cup sugar

½ teaspoon salt

1 lemon, juiced

Apple tart

½ cup (1 stick) butter

½ cup cream cheese

½ teaspoon salt

1½ cups flour

8 Granny Smith apples

Sugar

2 eggs

½ cup sugar

1 cup heavy cream

½ teaspoon ground nutmeg

½ teaspoon ground cinnamon

Salted or plain caramel sauce,
    for garnish

Dried apple chips, for garnish

Serves 6 to 8

Alsatian Apple Tart with Brown Butter Ice Cream

FRASER'S GOURMET HIDEAWAY, OAK HARBOR, WHIDBEY ISLAND
CHEF AND OWNER SCOTT FRASER

This could possibly be the most decadent ice cream recipe ever, starting with a custard base and then getting a flavor boost from brown butter. It's the perfect topping for the warm apple tart.

For the ice cream:

Heat a small pan over medium-high heat, melt the butter, and continue cooking until browned, about 5 minutes, taking care not to burn the milk solids. Cool the butter slightly, and then strain and discard the solids.

Combine the milk and cream in a medium saucepan over medium-high heat and heat to scalding. Beat the egg yolks and sugar together, and then add the butter, salt, and lemon juice and mix until incorporated. Whisk the hot milk into the yolks a little at a time until fully mixed. Return the mixture to the saucepan and cook, stirring frequently, until the mixture is thick enough to coat the back of a spoon, about 5 minutes. Place in the refrigerator to cool completely.

Freeze the mixture in an ice cream machine according to the manufacturer's directions, and then transfer to a covered container and freeze completely in the freezer.

For the apple tart:

Cream the butter, cheese, and salt together in a mixer or food processor. Add the flour and mix or pulse just until the dough comes together into a ball. Turn the dough out onto a lightly floured surface

(continued on page 152)

and pat into a thin round disk (the dough will be very soft). Press the dough into an 11-inch nonstick tart pan with a removable bottom, carefully pressing the dough evenly up the edges. Trim off any excess dough and place the tart pan on a baking sheet.

Preheat the oven to 350 degrees.

Peel, core, and quarter the apples. Place the apples into the tart shell, overlapping as you go, as the apples will shrink while they bake. Sprinkle with some sugar and bake for 20 minutes.

Whisk together the eggs, sugar, cream, nutmeg, and cinnamon and pour over the apples in the tart. Return the tart to the oven and cook until the custard is set, about 30 to 45 minutes. Cool the tart slightly before slicing and serving. Top tart slices with brown butter ice cream and garnish with caramel sauce and apple chips.

Apple-Cherry Bread Pudding

THE INN ON ORCAS ISLAND, DEER HARBOR, ORCAS ISLAND
INNKEEPER JEREMY TRUMBLE

Innkeeper Jeremy Trumble likes to serve this bread pudding after a hearty pork roast dinner, but admits that it's even better warmed and served left over as breakfast in bed.

3 eggs

1 cup plus 1 tablespoon sugar, divided

2 cups whole milk

1 cup heavy cream

2 teaspoons vanilla extract

1 teaspoon lemon zest

1 teaspoon ground cinnamon

3 crisp apples (like Jonagold or Pink Rose)

2 tablespoons butter

1 loaf day-old challah bread, cut into 2-inch cubes

½ cup dried cherries

1 cup slivered almonds, divided

Whipped cream or vanilla ice cream, for garnish

Serves 12

Preheat the oven to 350 degrees. Spray a 13 x 9 x 2-inch baking dish with cooking spray.

Combine the eggs with 1 cup of sugar in a mixing bowl and beat until fluffy, about 5 minutes. Add the milk, cream, vanilla, lemon zest, and cinnamon and mix well. Set aside.

Peel, core, and thinly slice the apples. Melt the butter in a large skillet over medium-high heat; add the apples and sauté for 2 to 3 minutes. Sprinkle with the remaining tablespoon of sugar and sauté until the sugar melts, about 1 to 2 more minutes.

Layer the bread, cherries, ¾ cup of the almonds, and apples in the baking dish in two layers. Pour the custard mixture over the top and press down on the ingredients so that everything is covered in the egg mixture. Top with the remaining almonds and bake, uncovered, until the custard is cooked through and the top nicely browned, about 45 minutes. Let stand for 10 minutes to set, then serve with whipped cream or ice cream.

¼ cup Meyers 151 rum

2 tablespoons banana liqueur

¾ cup (1½ sticks) butter

1 cup dark brown sugar

2 tablespoons freshly squeezed
lemon juice

4 medium ripe bananas, peeled
and cut lengthwise in half

1 pint vanilla bean ice cream

Serves 4

Bananas Foster

EL GAUCHO, SEATTLE
FOUNDER AND OWNER PAUL MACKAY
CORPORATE EXECUTIVE CHEF AND OWNER KEN SHARP

El Gaucho prepares this classic dessert tableside because it makes a nice show, but at home you'll love the simplicity of preparing it in just a couple of minutes right before serving.

Heat a large skillet over high heat and add the rum; carefully light to flambé and add the banana liqueur. Let flames burn off, then add the butter and swirl until melted. Add the brown sugar and stir until it completely dissolves and the mixture becomes thick and syrupy, about 3 to 5 minutes. Stir the lemon juice into the mixture, and then gently place the halved bananas in the skillet and cook until hot, about 1 to 2 minutes.

Scoop ice cream onto four dessert plates, place a banana half on each side of the ice cream, cover the bananas with the caramel sauce, and serve immediately.

Chocolate meringue hazelnuts

2 egg whites

1½ tablespoons sugar

2 tablespoons cocoa powder

2 cups hazelnuts

Cake base

1½ pounds Callebaut or other
    high-quality dark or
    semi-sweet chocolate

⅔ cup heavy cream

1 teaspoon salt

7 eggs, separated

⅔ cup sugar

⅔ cup caramel sauce

Chocolate tart

2¾ cup heavy cream, divided

½ pound Callebaut or other
    high-quality dark or
    semi-sweet chocolate

5 ounces mascarpone cheese,
    at room temperature

⅓ cup caramel sauce

Serves 12

Callebaut Chocolate Tart

WILD SAGE AMERICAN BISTRO, SPOKANE
CHEF GARE TRAEGER

*Although there are more than a few steps in this recipe, this stunning
chocolate tart is sure to delight guests.*

For the chocolate meringue hazelnuts:
Preheat the oven to 275 degrees. Line a baking sheet with parchment
paper.

Beat the egg whites in a mixing bowl until stiff peaks form, and
then add the sugar and cocoa powder. Continue mixing until the egg
whites are shiny and the ingredients are combined, about 30 seconds.
Fold in the hazelnuts by hand and pour the mixture onto the prepared baking sheet, spreading the nuts out into a single layer. Bake
until the meringue is dry, about 25 minutes.

Remove from the oven, and when cool, separate the nuts. Chop
half of the nuts and leave the remaining nuts whole for garnish.
Nuts may be made the day before and stored in a covered container.

For the cake base:
Preheat the oven to 350 degrees and spray a 9-inch springform pan
with cooking spray.

Melt the chocolate in the top of a double boiler set over medium-
high heat, stirring occasionally until melted, and then set aside.
Combine the cream with the salt and egg yolks in a mixing bowl
and mix until smooth. Fold in the melted chocolate.

In a separate mixing bowl, beat the egg whites until soft peaks form,
and then add the sugar and continue beating until stiff peaks form.
Fold the egg white mixture into the chocolate mixture, taking care not
to deflate the whites. Pour the mixture into the prepared pan, cover
with foil, and bake until a toothpick inserted into the center comes

(continued on page 156)

out clean, about 50 to 60 minutes. Remove the cake from the oven and cool (the cake may fall slightly as it cools).

After the cake has cooled, poke holes in the chocolate layer with a fork and spread the caramel sauce evenly over the cake. Sprinkle with the crushed chocolate meringue hazelnuts and refrigerate the cake for 2 hours.

For the chocolate tart:
Once the caramel layer has set, heat ¾ cup of the cream in a small saucepan over medium-high heat just until steaming. Remove from the heat, add the chocolate, and stir until the chocolate is fully incorporated to make the ganache. Let the ganache cool slightly, and then pour the melted ganache over the top of the chilled tart, gently spreading the ganache to cover the entire tart surface. Refrigerate until the ganache is firm and set, about 30 minutes.

When chilled, run a knife around the edge of the springform pan and release the tart, pushing the tart up from the bottom through the pan. Place the tart on a plate or cake stand.

Add the remaining 2 cups of cream to the bowl of a stand mixer and beat until stiff. Add the mascarpone cheese and caramel sauce and beat again until very stiff. Use a piping bag to pipe the caramel cream around the edge of the tart and place the remaining whole chocolate meringue hazelnuts on top of the tart. Serve extra whipped cream with slices of the tart.

Champagne Gelée "Bellini Dessert"

WILLCOX HOUSE COUNTRY INN, SEABECK, THE KITSAP PENINSULA
INNKEEPER CECELIA HUGHES

*Your guests will think they are enjoying a Bellini cocktail when you serve
this simple yet elegant dessert. At the inn, they use white peaches in the style
of a classic Italian Bellini, but yellow peaches look pretty in the glass.*

Soften the gelatin in cold water, and then warm the gelatin mixture
in a small saucepan on medium-low. Add ½ cup of the sugar; stir
until melted. Cool slightly in the refrigerator.

When cooled, pour the gelatin mixture into a medium bowl and
slowly stir in the Champagne. Refrigerate until the bubbles subside,
and then gently stir the mixture before refrigerating until set, at least
6 hours.

Peel and slice the peaches and toss with the remaining tablespoon
of sugar; let stand for 10 minutes for the sugar to melt.

To serve, alternate layers of the gelée and the peaches in four to six
wine glasses and garnish with sliced strawberries. May be held in
the refrigerator until ready to serve.

4 teaspoons gelatin
    (about 2 packets)

⅝ cup cold water

½ cup plus 1 tablespoon sugar,
    divided

1 bottle Champagne or Prosecco

Three peaches

Sliced strawberries, for garnish

Serves 4 to 6

1 cup cocoa powder

1¼ cup pastry flour
(see Guidelines for Recipes
on page xviii)

2½ cups sugar

1½ cups (3 sticks) butter

6 eggs

1 teaspoon vanilla extract

1½ cups roughly chopped walnuts

1½ cups chocolate chips

Yields 18 large brownies

Chocolate and Walnut Brownies

BIRCHFIELD MANOR COUNTRY HOUSE, YAKIMA
CHEF BRAD MASSET

Sheep farmers and senators have lived in this house prior to the Masset family buying it in 1978. Today the inn is a family affair, with Brad, who grew up here, taking the lead as chef.

Preheat the oven to 350 degrees. Spray a 13 x 9 x 2-inch baking dish with cooking spray. Sift together the cocoa powder and pastry flour and set aside.

Combine the sugar and butter in a mixing bowl and cream together until smooth, about 5 minutes. Slowly add the eggs and vanilla extract and mix until incorporated. With the mixer on low, add the cocoa powder and flour and mix just until incorporated. Stir in the walnuts and chocolate chips.

Spoon the brownie batter into the prepared baking dish and smooth the top. Bake until slightly set, but still a bit gooey in the center, about 40 to 50 minutes. Let brownies cool before slicing.

Christmas Tree Sherbet

THE HERBFARM RESTAURANT, WOODINVILLE
CHEF CHRIS WEBER

One of the nation's original farm-to-table restaurants, The Herbfarm creates twenty different nine-course menus throughout the year. Menus focus heavily on seasonal Pacific Northwest ingredients such as the edible needles of evergreen trees in this sherbet, which give it a woodsy, citrusy flavor to enjoy as an intermezzo or dessert. Although the sherbet is fun to serve during the holidays, it's enjoyable any time of the year.

1 cup sugar

3 cups water

4 cups evergreen needles
   (see Note)

¼ cup verjus or freshly squeezed
   lemon juice

¼ cup Champagne or dry
   white wine

¼ cup crème fraîche
   or heavy cream

Serves 16

Combine the sugar and water in a medium stockpot over medium-high heat and bring to a boil, stirring occasionally to dissolve the sugar. Add the evergreen needles, bring to a boil, remove from the heat, and cover. Steep the mixture for at least 45 minutes to fully infuse the flavor.

Strain the mixture and discard the needles. Add the verjus, Champagne, and crème fraîche to the infused liquid and whisk to combine. Chill the mixture fully in the refrigerator, and then freeze in an ice cream machine according to the manufacturer's directions. Store in a covered container in the freezer.

❧ **Note:** *The branch tips of fir and spruce trees have the best flavor. During the holidays you may use trimmings from your Christmas tree, but be sure your tree hasn't been treated with any chemical sprays.*

Lace cookies

½ cup (1 stick) butter

¾ cup sugar (preferably organic)

½ cup light corn syrup

1 teaspoon vanilla extract

½ teaspoon salt

⅓ cup flour

1 cup sliced almonds,
    finely chopped

1 tablespoon heavy cream

Pastry cream

2 eggs

¾ cup sugar

¼ cup cornstarch

2 cups whole milk

1 teaspoon vanilla extract

¼ teaspoon salt

Berries

2 pints fresh summer berries,
    any variety

Lemon verbena, lemon balm,
    or mint sprigs, for garnish

Serves 8

Cornets of Summer Berries

RESTAURANT MARCHÉ, BAINBRIDGE ISLAND
CHEF AND OWNER GREG ATKINSON

Summer berries are perfect in and of themselves, so Chef Atkinson prefers not to transform them into anything that diminishes their natural form. Instead, he creates a vessel for the berries—a delicate lace cookie cone—that showcases their subtle sweetness, and serves them with vanilla pastry cream.

For the lace cookies:

Heat the oven to 350 degrees. Line two baking sheet pans with silicone liners or parchment paper.

Melt the butter, sugar, and corn syrup in a medium saucepan over medium heat and cook while stirring for 5 to 6 minutes. Remove from the heat and stir in the vanilla, salt, flour, almonds, and cream; stir until smooth.

Use a ¼-cup measure to drop batter onto the cookie sheets. The cookies will spread as they heat, so plan on only 2 cookies per pan. Bake until the cookies are spread into thin, golden brown, lacey circles, about 7 to 8 minutes. Let the cookies cool and firm up slightly on the sheet pans for 1 to 2 minutes so that you can handle them, and then roll the cookies into cone shapes and cool to room temperature. Repeat, baking the remaining 4 cookies and shaping them into cones.

For the pastry cream:

Whisk the eggs, sugar, and cornstarch together in a large saucepan until smooth. Whisk in the milk and cook over medium–high heat, stirring constantly, until the mixture begins to boil, and then continue whisking until the foam subsides and the mixture thickens. Remove from the heat, stir in the vanilla and salt, and transfer the mixture to a shallow pan to cool. Cover with plastic wrap so the cream doesn't form a skin, and refrigerate until ready to serve.

To assemble:

Place a small dollop of pastry cream on each plate to anchor the cookie cones. Use a pastry bag or plastic bag with the corner snipped off to fill each cone with pastry cream. Pile berries at the mouth of the cones, distributing the berries evenly among the serving plates. Garnish with sprigs of lemon verbena, lemon balm, or mint and serve immediately.

Fig layer

4 cups dried black mission figs

4 tablespoons butter, softened

¾ cup brown sugar

1½ teaspoons salt

Cake

1½ cups sweet rice flour
   (see Sources on page 174)

1¼ cups sugar

1 teaspoon baking powder

⅛ teaspoon salt

2 tablespoons milk

3 eggs

2 tablespoons melted butter

1 tablespoon vanilla extract

Chinese sausage crumble

6 tablespoons cold butter, cubed

¾ cup plus 2 tablespoons
   sweet rice flour

2 tablespoons brown sugar

¼ cup sugar

1 cup peeled and ground Chinese
   sausage or cooked and
   minced chorizo sausage
   (see Sources on page 174)

Fig Upside Down Cake

JOULE, SEATTLE ❧ CHEF RACHEL YANG AND CHEF SEIF CHIRCHI

This dense fig cake resembles a giant fig newton cookie and is served at Joule with a blue cheese whipped topping and Chinese sausage crumbles that bring really unique sweet and savory flavors to the cake. If pressed for time, or for simplicity, the cake is equally good with a simple garnish of whipped cream.

For the fig layer:
Grease a 13 x 9 x 2-inch baking dish, place a piece of parchment paper in the bottom, and grease the paper as well.

Remove the stems from the figs. Slice figs and soak in hot water until they are soft, about 20 minutes; drain and discard the soaking liquid.

Cream together the butter, sugar, and salt in a stand mixer until combined. Add the softened figs, gently mix together, and then spread the mixture in the bottom of the prepared pan.

For the cake:
Preheat the oven to 375 degrees.

Combine the rice flour, sugar, baking powder, salt, milk, eggs, melted butter, and vanilla in a mixing bowl and beat until smooth. Pour the batter over the fig mixture. Bake until the cake is golden brown and set, about 30 to 45 minutes, and then chill the cake completely in the refrigerator.

For the Chinese sausage crumble:
Preheat the oven to 350 degrees. Combine the butter, flour, brown sugar, sugar, and sausage and use your fingers to crumb the mixture together until small clumps form. Spread the mixture on a rimmed baking sheet and bake until golden brown, about 15 minutes.

For the blue cheese whipped topping:

Blue cheese whipped topping

½ cup Gorgonzola crumbles

½ cup powdered sugar

½ tablespoon vanilla extract

¼ cup heavy cream

¾ cup mascarpone cheese

Serves 12

Combine the Gorgonzola, sugar, and vanilla in a mixing bowl and beat together. Add the cream and mascarpone and beat until smooth and thick.

To serve:
Carefully invert the cooled cake onto a flat surface and cut into individual pieces. Garnish the cake slices with a dollop of the blue cheese whipped topping and sprinkle with the Chinese sausage crumble. Alternatively, serve with whipped cream.

Candied bacon

¾ pound bacon

¼ cup brown sugar

¼ teaspoon pepper

Cream cheese frosting

1 cup (2 sticks) unsalted butter, softened

1 (8-ounce) package cream cheese, softened

4 cups powdered sugar

2 teaspoons vanilla extract

2 teaspoons honey

Cake

2½ cups flour

1 tablespoon baking powder

1 tablespoon ground ginger

½ tablespoon ground cinnamon

¼ teaspoon ground cloves

½ teaspoon salt

1½ cups boiling water

1 cup honey

1 teaspoon baking soda

1 cup (2 sticks) unsalted butter, at room temperature, plus more for buttering the pan

1 cup packed brown sugar

1 egg

¼ cup finely grated fresh ginger

Serves 8 to 12

Ginger Cake with Cream Cheese Frosting and Candied Bacon

MAXWELL'S, TACOMA   ❧   CHEF HUDSON SLATER

By pairing classic cream cheese frosting with candied bacon, not to mention a healthy dose of fresh ginger, Chef Slater has created an irresistible cake bursting with intense flavors. He uses local honey in the cake and serves it warm in the restaurant.

For the candied bacon:
Preheat the oven to 425 degrees. Place a wire rack over a rimmed baking sheet and spray with nonstick cooking spray.

Coat each piece of bacon with brown sugar on both sides, and then place the coated bacon pieces on the wire rack. Sprinkle with pepper and bake until the bacon is caramelized and crispy, about 15 to 20 minutes. Watch closely, as the sugar can begin to burn quickly once the bacon is cooked. Remove from the oven, let cool, chop, and set aside.

For the cream cheese frosting:
Combine the butter and cream cheese in a large mixing bowl and beat together until smooth. With the mixer on low speed, add the powdered sugar 1 cup at a time until smooth and creamy, and then beat in the vanilla extract and honey.

For the cake:
Set a rack in the center of the oven and preheat the oven to 325 degrees. Generously butter the sides and bottom of two (8-inch) round metal baking pans or a 13 x 9 x 2-inch glass baking dish, and line the bottom with parchment paper.

Combine the flour, baking powder, ground ginger, cinnamon, cloves, and salt in a large bowl and whisk together; set aside. Combine the boiling water, honey, and baking soda in a small saucepan over medium-high heat and cook until the honey has completely dissolved.

Place the butter and brown sugar in a mixing bowl and use the paddle attachment to mix on high speed until light and fluffy, about 3 minutes, scraping down the sides of the bowl as necessary. Reduce the speed to medium-low, add the egg, and mix until combined. Add the grated ginger and mix to combine.

Add the flour mixture in three increments, alternating with the honey mixture, scraping down the sides as necessary. The batter will be very wet and loose. Pour the batter into the prepared pans and transfer to the oven. Bake until a toothpick inserted into the center of the cake comes out clean, about 45 minutes to 1 hour. Let cool to room temperature, turn onto a wire rack or dish, and then frost and sprinkle with candied bacon pieces.

Crust

1 cup ground toasted pecans

1 cup brown sugar

4 cups graham cracker crumbs

1 teaspoon cinnamon

1 teaspoon nutmeg

1 cup (2 sticks) butter, melted

Filling

5 (8-ounce) packages cream
    cheese, at room temperature

2 cups sugar

2 vanilla beans

2 cups heavy cream

3 lemons, zested and juiced

4 eggs

3 egg yolks

Serves 12

Lemon Vanilla Cheesecake

CAFE NOLA, BAINBRIDGE ISLAND
CHEF AND OWNER KEVIN WARREN

Chef Warren creates artfully designed plates from seasonal ingredients in his European-style bistro just a short ferry ride from Seattle. This cheesecake has a light texture to it even though the flavor is very dense. Bake it uncovered if you want to brown the top, or cover it while baking if you prefer it not to brown.

For the crust:
Prepare a 10-inch springform pan by wrapping it in 2 to 3 layers of heavy-duty aluminum foil so that the pan is watertight, and then place the prepared pan in a roasting pan. Preheat the oven to 450 degrees.

Combine the pecans, brown sugar, graham cracker crumbs, cinnamon, and nutmeg in a medium bowl. Stir in the melted butter to make a crumbly texture. Press the crust into the bottom of the prepared pan, pressing the crust ½ to 1 inch up the sides of the pan; set aside.

For the filling:
Add the cream cheese to the bowl of a food processor and process slightly. Add the sugar and pulse to combine until the mixture is creamy. Transfer the mixture to a mixing bowl.

Cut the vanilla beans in half lengthwise and scrape the seeds into the cream cheese mixture. With the mixer on low and using the paddle blade, add the cream, lemon zest, and lemon juice and mix until smooth. Add the eggs and egg yolks one at a time and continue to mix on low just until incorporated. Do not over mix to avoid excess air in the batter.

To assemble:
Pour the filling into the prepared crust (the filling will reach very close to the top of the pan). Add hot water into the roasting pan around the springform pan to create a water bath. Place the entire roasting pan in the oven for 30 minutes. After 30 minutes, turn off the oven, do not open the door, and allow the cheesecake to sit in the oven at least 6 hours or overnight. Remove the cake from the oven and refrigerate until completely cold, 4 or more hours, before slicing and serving.

Cake

½ cup Chateau Ste. Michelle
Muscat Canelli wine
(see Sources on page 174)

½ cup chopped dried sour cherries

¾ cup yellow raisins

1 cup (2 sticks) unsalted butter,
softened

2¾ cups superfine sugar

6 eggs

1 cup sour cream

1 tablespoon vanilla extract

3 cups cake flour
*(see Guidelines for Recipes
on page xviii)*

1 ½ teaspoon baking soda

1 teaspoon cinnamon

½ teaspoon ground nutmeg

⅛ teaspoon ground cloves

½ teaspoon ground cardamom

½ teaspoon ground ginger

¾ cup chopped pecans

Glaze

1 cup powdered sugar, sifted

3 tablespoons Chateau
Ste. Michelle Muscat
Canelli wine

2 tablespoons honey

1 teaspoon vanilla extract

Yields 2 loaves

Muscat Canelli Pound Cake

CHATEAU STE. MICHELLE, WOODINVILLE　❧　CHEF JOHN SARICH

Chateau Ste. Michelle is the oldest winery in Washington, and Chef Sarich creates interesting recipes that showcase their wine, like this sweet and floral pound cake. His creations naturally pair well with wines from the winery, and he recommends serving this dessert with Chateau Ste. Michelle's Late Harvest Chenin Blanc wine.

For the cake:
Preheat the oven to 350 degrees. Butter and flour two 9 x 5 x 3-inch loaf pans (1-quart size).

Combine the Chateau Ste. Michelle Muscat Canelli, cherries, and raisins in a small bowl and set aside.

Place the butter and sugar in a mixing bowl and cream until light and fluffy, about 5 minutes. Add the eggs 1 at a time, making sure each is incorporated before adding the next. Add the sour cream and vanilla and beat well, scraping down the sides as needed.

Combine the flour, baking soda, cinnamon, nutmeg, cloves, cardamom, and ginger in a bowl and whisk until well mixed. Slowly add the dry ingredients to the mixing bowl and beat on low just until combined. Fold in the pecans and the cherry mixture and divide evenly between the prepared pans, smoothing the tops.

Bake until a skewer inserted in the center comes out clean, about 50 to 60 minutes, covering with foil during the last 10 minutes to prevent the tops from over-browning. Remove from the oven, uncover, and cool for 30 minutes. Remove the cakes from the pans and finish cooling on a wire rack, about 30 more minutes.

For the glaze:
Place the sugar, wine, honey, and vanilla in a small bowl, and use a whisk to mix until completely combined. Drizzle the glaze evenly over the two cooled cakes.

Poached pears

1 bottle red wine

¾ cup sugar

1 orange, peeled in strips, no pith

1 cinnamon stick

1 vanilla bean, sliced lengthwise

3 whole star anise

2 whole cloves

1 teaspoon black peppercorns

4 pears, peeled, halved,
    and cored

Almond crust

3¼ cups almond flour

½ cup plus 2 tablespoons sugar

½ teaspoon baking soda

½ teaspoon sea salt

1 tablespoon ground cinnamon

1 teaspoon ground cardamom

¼ cup canola oil

2 tablespoons water

(continued on page 170)

Red Wine
Poached Pear Clafoutis

THE MARC, THE MARCUS WHITMAN HOTEL, WALLA WALLA
EXECUTIVE CHEF ANTONIO CAMPOLIO

Chef Campolio's culinary journey began in his family restaurant as a child and continued through a variety of restaurant experiences, including distinguished venues such as the Greenbriar Hotel in West Virginia and the Broadmoor Hotel in Colorado, before he became the Executive Chef at The Marc. He has won multiple culinary honors, and in 2012 was invited to prepare a Walla Walla-themed menu at the prestigious James Beard House.

For the poached pears:
Combine the wine, sugar, orange peel, cinnamon, vanilla bean, anise, cloves, peppercorns, and pear halves in a medium saucepan. Cut a 1-inch hole in the center of a circle of parchment paper (to release steam) and place it over the ingredients in the pot. Cook over medium-low heat until the pears are fork tender, about an hour. Drain the pears and allow them to cool.

For the almond crust:
Preheat the oven to 325 degrees.

Whisk the almond flour, sugar, baking soda, salt, cinnamon, and cardamom together in a large bowl. Add the oil and water and stir with a spoon to combine. Knead the dough with your hands until well combined. Press into an 11-inch tart pan with a removable bottom, pressing the crust all the way up the sides. Bake the crust until lightly browned, about 10 minutes. Remove from the oven and set aside.

(continued on page 170)

Filling

¼ cup sugar

2 eggs

½ cup heavy cream

2 teaspoons pear brandy
    or other brandy

½ tablespoon vanilla extract

2 tablespoons melted butter

¼ cup almond flour

Serves 6 to 8

For the filling:
Combine the sugar, eggs, cream, brandy, vanilla, melted butter, and almond flour in a blender and blend until smooth, about 15 seconds.

To assemble the clafoutis:
Preheat the oven to 350 degrees. Slice the poached pears and lay the pear slices in attractive layers on the bottom of the tart crust. Pour the egg mixture over the top and bake until fully set and slightly puffy, about 30 to 40 minutes. Serve warm, or refrigerate.

Ganache

¼ cup heavy cream

2 ounces milk chocolate, chopped

Cake

1 ounce bittersweet chocolate,
    chopped

1 ounce milk chocolate, chopped

1 egg

1 egg yolk

Pinch sugar

2 tablespoons butter

2 tablespoons sugar

1 tablespoon water

1 tablespoon flour

Pinch salt

Chocolate shavings, for garnish

Chantilly cream

6½ tablespoons heavy cream

2 tablespoons powdered sugar,
    sifted

2 tablespoons shaved
    bittersweet chocolate

Serves 4

Theo Chocolate Ganache Cake

TILTH, SEATTLE   ❧   CHEF AND OWNER MARIA HINES

James Beard award-winning Chef Maria Hines has created a small restaurant empire in the Seattle area. She uses chocolate from Seattle-based chocolatier Theo in this rich dessert, and recommends pairing the cake with Domaine Piétri Géraud Banyuls dessert wine.

For the ganache:
Heat the cream over a double boiler and slowly whisk in the chopped chocolate until completely melted. Remove from the heat and chill in the refrigerator until slightly firm.

For the cake:
Place the bittersweet and milk chocolate in a small bowl and set aside. Combine the egg, egg yolk, and pinch of sugar in a large mixing bowl and mix using the whisk attachment until the mixture forms thick ribbons, about 10 minutes.

While the eggs are whisking, combine the butter, 2 tablespoons of sugar, and water in a small saucepan over medium-high heat and bring to a boil. Reduce the heat and simmer until the butter is melted. Pour the hot mixture over the chocolate and stir until the chocolate is melted and well blended. Add the melted chocolate to the eggs and stir until incorporated. Stir in the flour and salt; refrigerate at least 1 hour, or up to overnight.

Preheat the oven to 350 degrees.

Roll the ganache into 4 balls. Fill four 3-ounce silicone cake molds one-third full with batter and place a ball of ganache in the center of each cake. Divide the remaining batter evenly among the 4 cakes to cover the ganache and smooth the tops. Bake until the sides are set and the tops puff, but the cakes are still soft, about 15 to 17 minutes. Let cool for 2 minutes, and then invert the cakes onto a sheet pan to cool completely.

(continued on page 172)

For the Chantilly cream:
When you are ready to serve the cakes, whisk the cream until soft peaks form, and then whisk in the powdered sugar and chopped chocolate.

Presentation:
Place the cakes on the center of small dessert plates and top with a small dollop of the Chantilly cream. Garnish with chocolate shavings and serve.

1 pint heavy cream

1 cup half-and-half

½ vanilla bean

5 egg yolks

2 eggs

½ cup sugar

½ teaspoon salt

Serves 4

Vanilla Bean Crème Brûlée

THE MARC, THE MARCUS WHITMAN HOTEL, WALLA WALLA
EXECUTIVE CHEF ANTONIO CAMPOLIO

*Crème brûlée is always a popular dessert, and is quite simple to make.
Either sprinkle a bit of sugar on top and brown with a kitchen torch,
or top with your favorite berries before serving.*

Preheat the oven to 350 degrees. Place four 8-ounce custard
dishes into a shallow pan and set aside.

Combine the heavy cream, half-and-half, and vanilla bean in
a medium saucepan over medium-high heat and heat until just
below simmering.

Whisk the egg yolks, eggs, and sugar together in a large bowl until
well combined. Slowly whisk small amounts of the hot liquid into
the eggs a little at a time until fully incorporated, and then stir in
the salt.

Strain the mixture with a fine mesh strainer to remove any lumps,
and then divide the mixture evenly among the four custard dishes.
Add water to the pan around the custard dishes to come about
halfway up the sides, and then cover the entire pan with foil. Bake
until set, about 30 to 40 minutes. When the custards jiggle but
remain as one, they are done. Chill the crème brûlée before serving.

sources for specialty ingredients and other products

Beecher's Handmade Cheese: at Beecher's Handmade Cheese at Pike Place Market in Seattle or online at beechershandmadecheese.com

Beef Glacé: in fine food stores or online at amazon.com

Beluga Lentils: in fine food stores or online at igourmet.com

Bragg Liquid Aminos: in grocery stores or online at bragg.com

Chateau Ste. Michelle Muscat Canelli wine: in wine shops or directly from the winery in Woodinville

Chinese Sausage: in Asian grocery stores or online at efooddepot.com

Duck Confit: from specialty butchers or online at dartagnan.com

Gaucho Steak Seasoning: in El Gaucho restaurants or online at elgaucho.com

Geoduck Clams: at Pike Place Market, any of the Taylor Shellfish retail stores (call ahead to place your order), or online at taylorshellfishfarms.com

Joseph's Grainery Lentils: in many grocery stores and markets across Washington or online at josephsgrainery.com

Kecap Manis: in Asian grocery stores or online at amazon.com

Kombu: at Whole Foods or online at edenfoods.com

Korean Salted Shrimp: in H Mart stores or online at hmart.com

Lapsang Souchong Tea: in grocery stores or online at amazon.com

Lavender: at Penzeys Spices in Seattle or online at penzeys.com

Marcona Almonds: at Costco, Whole Foods, or online at nuts.com

Minor's Crab Base: in grocery stores or online at amazon.com

Preserved Lemons: at Whole Foods (in the prepared foods area) or online at williams-sonoma.com or surlatable.com

Shellfish: at any of the Taylor Shellfish retail stores (call ahead to place your order) or online at taylorshellfishfarms.com

Spices: at Penzeys Spices in Seattle or online at penzeys.com

Steen's Cane Syrup: at The Wandering Goose in Seattle or online at steensyrup.com

Sweet Rice Flour: in grocery stores (with the specialty flours) or online at bobsredmill.com

contributors

Abendblume
12570 Ranger Road
Leavenworth, WA 98826
800-669-7634
info@abendblume.com
abendblume.com

Altura
617 Broadway Avenue East
Seattle, WA 98102
206-402-6749
info@alturarestaurant.com
alturarestaurant.com

AQUA by El Gaucho
2801 Alaskan Way, Pier 70
Seattle, WA 98121
206-956-9171
tamara@elgaucho.com
elgaucho.com

Backdoor Kitchen
400 A Street
Friday Harbor, San Juan Island, WA 98250
360-378-9540
hilderman@rockisland.com
backdoorkitchen.com

Barking Frog, Willows Lodge
14580 NE 145th Street
Woodinville, WA 98072
425-424-3900 - Willows Lodge
425-424-2999 - Barking Frog
mail@willowslodge.com
willowslodge.com/barking_frog/

The Bay Café
9 Old Post Road
Lopez Island, WA 98261
360-468-3700
tim@bay-cafe.com
bay-cafe.com

Bennett's
7650 SE 27th Street
Mercer Island, WA 98040
206-232-2759
thestaff@bennettsbistro.com
bennettsbistro.com

Birchfield Manor Country House
2018 Birchfield Road
Yakima, WA 98901
509-452-1960
info@birchfieldmanor.com
birchfieldmanor.com

Blind Pig Bistro
2238 Eastlake Avenue
Seattle, WA 98102
206-329-2744
sweetbreads@comcast.net
blindpigbistro.com

**Bonneville Hot Springs Resort
and Spa**
1252 East Cascade Drive
North Bonneville, WA 98639
866-459-1678
reservations@bhsr.us
bonnevilleresort.com

Café Flora
2901 East Madison Street
Seattle, WA 98112
206-325-9100
info@cafeflora.com
cafeflora.com

Cafe Nola
101 Winslow Way East
Bainbridge Island, WA 98110
206-842-3822
info@cafenola.com
cafenola.com

Canlis
2576 Aurora Avenue North
Seattle, WA 98109
206-283-3313
canlis@canlis.com
canlis.com

Chateau Ste. Michelle
14111 NE 145th Street
Woodinville, WA 98072
425-488-1133
info@ste-michelle.com
ste-michelle.com

Cherry Chalet Bed and Breakfast
8101 West 10th
Kennewick, WA 99336
509-308-7203
steve@cherrychalet.com
cherrychalet.com

Chinaberry Hill
302 Tacoma Avenue North
Tacoma, WA 98403
253-272-1282
chinaberry@wa.net
chinaberryhill.com

Christopher's on Whidbey
103 NW Coveland Street
Coupeville, WA 98239
360-678-5480
christophersonwhidbey@comcast.net
christophersonwhidbey.com

Crush
2319 East Madison Street
Seattle, WA 98112
206-302-7874
nicole@chefjasonwilson.com
chefjasonwilson.com

El Gaucho
2505 First Avenue
Seattle, WA 98121
(locations also in Bellevue,
Tacoma, and Portland, Oregon)
206-728-1337
tamara@elgaucho.com
elgaucho.com

Fraser's Gourmet Hideaway
1191 SE Dock Street #101
Oak Harbor, Whidbey Island, WA 98277
360-279-1231
frasersgh@comcast.net
frasersgh.com

Gordon's on Blueberry Hill
5438 South Woodard Avenue
Freeland, WA 98249
360-331-7515
gordonsonblueberryhill@gmail.com
gordonsonblueberryhill.com

The Greenlake Guest House
7630 East Green Lake Drive North
Seattle, WA 98103
206-729-8700 or 866-355-8700
stay@greenlakeguesthouse.com
greenlakeguesthouse.com

A Harbor View Inn
111 West 11th Street
Aberdeen, WA, 98520
360-533-7996 or 877-533-7996
info@aharborview.com
aharborview.com

The Herbfarm Restaurant
14590 NE 145th Street
Woodinville, WA 98072
425-485-5300
rosemary@theherbfarm.com
theherbfarm.com

How to Cook a Wolf
2208 Queen Anne Avenue North
Seattle, WA 98109
206-838-8090
info@ethanstowellrestaurants.com
ethanstowellrestaurants.com/
howtocookawolf/

Il Terrazzo Carmine
411 1st Avenue South
Seattle, WA 98104
206-467-7797
carminesseattle@gmail.com
ilterrazzocarmine.com

The Inn on Orcas Island
114 Channel Road
Deer Harbor, WA 98243
888-886-1661
jeremy@theinnonorcasisland.com
theinnonorcasisland.com

Joseph's Grainery
PO Box 662
Colfax, WA 99111
509-397-3670
info@josephsgrainery.com
josephsgrainery.com

Joule
3506 Stone Way North
Seattle, WA 98103
206-632-5685
info@joulerestaurant.com
joulerestaurant.com

Keenan's at the Pier
The Chrysalis Inn and Spa
804 10th Street
Bellingham, WA 98225
888-808-0005
reservations@thechrysalisinn.com
thechrysalisinn.com

La Medusa
4857 Rainier Avenue South
Seattle, WA 98118
206-723-2192
info@lamedusarestaurant.com
lamedusarestaurant.com

Lake Quinault Lodge
345 South Shore Road
Quinault, WA 98575
360-288-2900 or 800-562-6672
beck-paula@aramark.com
olympicnationalparks.com/
accommodations/lake-quinault-lodge.aspx

Le Pichet
1933 1st Avenue
Seattle, WA 98101
206-256-1499
info@lepichetseattle.com
lepichetseattle.com

Lisa Nakamura
lisaknakamura@gmail.com
gnocchibarseattle.com

LloydMartin
1525 Queen Anne North
Seattle, WA 98109
206-420-7602
chefsamcrannell@gmail.com
lloydmartinseattle.com

Luc
2800 East Madison
Seattle, WA 98112
206-328-6645
info@thechefinthehat.com
thechefinthehat.com/luc/

Luna
5620 South Perry Street
Spokane, WA 99223
509-448-2383
info@lunaspokane.com
lunaspokane.com

The Marc
The Marcus Whitman Hotel
6 West Rose Street
Walla Walla, WA 99362
509-524-5118
execchef@mwhcc.com
marcuswhitmanhotel.com/the-marc

Matt's in the Market
94 Pike Street
Seattle, WA 98101
206-467-7909
shane@mattsinthemarket.com
mattsinthemarket.com

Maxwell's
454 St. Helens Avenue
Tacoma, WA 98402
253-683-4115
info@maxwells-tacoma.com
maxwells-tacoma.com

Pike Place Chowder
1530 Post Alley
Seattle, WA 98101
206-267-2537
info@pikeplacechowder.com
pikeplacechowder.com

Plum Bistro
1429 12th Avenue
Seattle, WA 98122
206-838-5333
info@plumbistro.com
plumbistro.com

Poppy
622 Broadway East
Seattle, WA 98102
206-324-1108
info@poppyseattle.com
poppyseattle.com

Prima Bistro
201½ First Street
Langley, WA 98260
360-221-4060
primabistro@whidbey.com
primabistro.com

Restaurant Marché
150 Madrone Lane North
Bainbridge Island, WA 98110
206-842-1633
greg@restaurantmarchebainbridge.com
restaurantmarchebainbridge.com

Revel
403 North 36th Street
Seattle, WA 98103
206-547-2040
info@revelseattle.com
revelseattle.com

Run of the River Inn & Refuge
9308 East Leavenworth Road
Leavenworth, WA 98826
800-288-6491
info@runoftheriver.com
runoftheriver.com

Saffron Mediterranean Kitchen
125 West Alder Street
Walla Walla, WA 99362
509-525-2112
saffronmediterraneankitchen.com

Shanik
#500 Terry Avenue North
Seattle, WA 98109
206-486-6884
contact@shanikrestaurant.com
shanikrestaurant.com

The Shelburne Inn
4415 Pacific Way
Seaview, WA 98644
360-642-2442
frontdesk@theshelburneinn.com
theshelburneinn.com

Six Seven Restaurant
The Edgewater Hotel
2411 Alaskan Way, Pier 67
Seattle, WA 98121
206-728-7000
dining@edgewaterhotel.com
edgewaterhotel.com/seattle-six-
seven-restaurant.aspx

Staple & Fancy Mercantile
4739 Ballard Avenue NW
Seattle, WA 98107
206-789-1200
info@ethanstowellrestaurants.com
ethanstowellrestaurants.com/
stapleandfancy/

Sushi Kappo Tamura
2968 Eastlake Avenue East
Seattle, WA 98102
206-547-0937
info@sushikappotamura.com
sushikappotamura.com

Sutra
1605 North 45th Street
Seattle, WA 98103
206-547-1348
sutraseattle@gmail.com
sutraseattle.com

Swantown Inn
1431 11th Avenue SE
Olympia, WA 98501
360-753-9123
yourhosts@swantowninn.com
swantowninn.com

Tilth
1411 North 45th Street
Seattle, WA 98103
206-633-0801
info@tilthrestaurant.com
tilthrestaurant.com

Trace
1112 4th Avenue
Seattle, WA 98101
206-264-6060
TraceSeattle@Whotels.com
traceseattle.com

Twigs Bistro and Martini Bar
Multiple locations across
WA, OR, UT, and ID including:
1321 North Columbia Center Boulevard
Suite 901A
Kennewick, WA 99336
509-735-3411
kennewick@twigsbistro.com
twigsbistro.com

Volunteer Park Cafe
1501 17th Avenue East
Seattle, WA 98112
206-328-3155
info@alwaysfreshgoodness.com
alwaysfreshgoodness.com

The Wandering Goose
403 15th Avenue East
Seattle, WA 98112
206-323-9938
info@thewanderinggoose.com
thewanderinggoose.com

Westward
2501 North Northlake Way
Seattle, WA 98103
206-552-8215
ahoy@westwardseattle.com
westwardseattle.com

Whitehouse–Crawford Restaurant
55 West Cherry Street
Walla Walla, WA 99362
509-525-2222
manager@whitehousecrawford.com
whitehousecrawford.com

Whoopemup Hollow Café
120 Main Street
Waitsburg, WA 99361
509-337-9000
info@whoopemuphollowcafe.com
whoopemuphollowcafe.com

The Wild Iris Inn
121 Maple Avenue
La Conner, WA 98257
360-466-1400
lfarnell@wildiris.com
wildiris.com

Wild Sage American Bistro
916 West 2nd Avenue
Spokane, WA 99201
509-456-7575
tom@wildsagebistro.com
wildsagebistro.com

Willcox House Country Inn
2390 Tekiu Point Road NW
Seabeck, WA 98380
800-725-9477 or 360-830-4492
willcoxhouse@silverlink.net
willcoxhouse.com

index

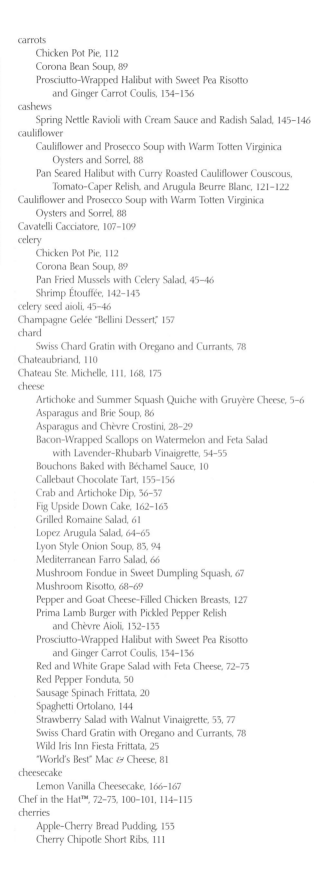